Worship
For
Today

WORSHIP FOR TODAY

Suggestions and Ideas

EDITED BY
RICHARD JONES

EPWORTH PRESS

© RICHARD JONES 1968
FIRST PUBLISHED IN 1968
BY EPWORTH PRESS
Book Steward: Frank Cumbers
SBN 7162 0035 X
PRINTED IN GREAT BRITAIN
BY PAGE & THOMAS LTD
CHESHAM, BUCKINGHAMSHIRE

Contents

Preface

ANY situation which compels a section of the Methodist Establishment at Westminster to join hands with the organized *avant garde* must be reckoned a serious one. The need for the renewal of Methodist worship in the direction of more effective communication and greater relevance to the life of the secular world is such a situation.

Three out of four Methodist Sunday services are conducted by Local Preachers. If this book encourages them (and others) to make experiments in worship and at the same time saves them from that gimmickry which is the occupational disease of those who experiment, then it will have been good that the Local Preachers Department and the Renewal Group made common cause.

JOHN STACEY
Secretary
Local Preachers Department
1 *Central Buildings, London, S.W.*1

Preface

Introduction

AMIDST all the current clamour for the renewal of the Church, which we must surely attribute to the zeal of God, the cry for a renewal of her worship sounds with increasing urgency. It is not simply the cry of the young who, in their naivety, want more bright gimmicks. It is not simply the cry of those who want an entertainment every Sunday, nor does it come because some people are wearied by the minister. It is not simply the cry of those restless and rootless souls (spiritual hippies?) for whom order and stability are anathema. If it were, we could dismiss it all with a shrug and a few pious admonitions. Instead, it is a cry of genuine agony born out of deep pain within the heart of modern Christian. He longs to rejoice in the gospel, he yearns for a new vision of the glory of God, he hungers for an authentic word from God which will make immediate impact within his new manner of life. New it is, within a world increasingly secular and less and less conscious of God.

With growing conviction and unanimity he tells us that our usual patterns of worship are inadequate and are starving his soul. He is not helped if we reply that these patterns served our grandparents well in the great heyday of Church-going around the turn of the century. God has moved mankind forward by many paces since then. He is not helped if we offer to brighten up the hymns, rearrange the prayers, adopt a snippet of 'liturgy' or shorten the sermon, for all these measures are superficial and both he and we know it.

He is only slightly helped if we offer to expound the basic principles of our traditional worship pattern. This may merely confirm his suspicion that the modern Church simply will not recognize the tensions of the contemporary Christian for what they are. So, if we point out that our worship is built around the proclamation of the word of God through the sermon by a trained expositor of the Bible, he will comment that this requires an equal sensitivity to the nature of the modern world as to the nature of Scripture before that word is to have a cutting edge, and that in his experience this rarely happens. The preacher seems to live in another world understandable only in thought-forms which are inappropriate to those pertaining within contemporary life, so his inspired utterance ends up as a holy irrelevance. Moreover he finds that truth presented to him in one unambiguous and unchallengeable statement is rarely satisfying because truth is often complex. He discovers its authority more and more within dialogue between contrasts, just as he can only see the depth of distance within any vista by using his two eyes, viewing from slightly contrasting positions.

If we point out that Christian worship centres upon the sermon or spoken word, he may well complain in addition that this inevitably makes our worship into an intellectual activity, too dependent upon words and listening, upon thought and concentration. He will want to know if worship *must* be built around speech and mental attention. Is there not some justification for requiring worship to be built around movement, drama, and symbol? He may well note that Jesus deliberately commanded His people to observe certain *actions*, like baptizing with water or eating bread and drinking wine.

More importantly still, he may be querying the mood of our worship. Does God require of us a solemn assembly, grave speech and awed listening, the excessive grovelling of our confessions of sin ('miserable offenders',[1] 'no health in us'), our apparent concentration upon just those aspects of the work of Christ which relate to the human 'plight' (salvation, atonement, justification, redemption), the preacher draped in black, the people forced upright by stiff pews, the pattern of the service rigid like the laws of the Medes and Persians, the surroundings dominated by varnished oak and pitch pine? Behind this query about mood lie basic questions about the gospel. Is it to be understood primarily as good news that in Christ God has acted to rescue us from our sins, or is its essence more positive, to wit, that God is incredible love, accepting us in Christ, transforming us and all creation? As the consensus of Christian opinion moves subtly to give preference to the second answer, there emerges a noticeably fresh understanding of the basic meaning of our worship. That is, Christian worship is *celebration* of the gospel. Its key-note is not its solemnity, nor the emotional state it can induce in the worshipper (to make him feel 'better'), nor the declamation it can produce upon man's sin—but its exultation in the magnificent news that this is God's world despite all appearance to the contrary, that He is the love made plain in Christ, that we can live in and for Him.

But there is yet more to be said about the characteristic mood of our worship, for here we touch upon the major theological concerns of the day. How are we to understand God's dealings with us and our world? The modern scientific world-view makes it increasingly difficult for us to conceive God as a great power encircling the world, able to inject his influences into it whenever possible 'from above'. The Greeks found this method of thinking quite congenial and so, traditionally, have Christians. Our grandparents envisaged their lives as a sequence of experiences in which this 'in-break' occurred, and by which they were sustained in their constant struggle against

[1]The original meaning was 'in dire need of forgiveness', of course. Nowadays it too often appears to be an apt description of our emotional state.

the devil and all His works. Their prayers were passionate pleas for God's intervention from His holy state into our sinful, chaotic existence. Worship expressed their entreaty that God should come and act, and the high moments of emotional intensity within the service were interpreted as convincing demonstrations that He had done. It is not simply that elementary psychology has undermined this belief, but that this relation between God's transcendence and our earthly existence is being radically queried. The result is a widespread (but often secret) abandonment of the practice of prayer, a disenchantment with traditional patterns of worship and spirituality, and a major theological turmoil.

Whilst this turmoil causes its reverberations throughout our Church life there are, of course, many voices urging us to standardize our worship, to retain some stability despite all the flux of modern man's life and thought, to hold firm to venerable and well-tried patterns like those of the Book of Common Prayer, and hence to cultivate what is loosely termed 'the liturgical'. If the modern Liturgical Movement leads to such conservatism it will become a major and tragic obstacle to the renewal of the Church. We would find ourselves subjecting the human spirit to yet another rigid tyranny at precisely the moment when it is crying for liberation and fresh air. It would replace our yearning for a living, vibrant worship by a scrupulous regard for the minutiae of liturgical scholarship and an obsession with the spiritual fossils of the Church's past. But the Liturgical Movement is not meant to be turned into an excuse for retreat into an obscure and uncongenial past. Within it there are genuine insights which are vital to the future health of the Church. It insists, for example, that worship be carefully and deliberately *ordered*, that it expresses the corporate offering of the whole people of God (not merely the clerics), that we treat the Holy Communion as the classic type of Christian celebration. These insights are precious indeed, even if their application necessitates major upheaval in normal Anglican as well as nonconformist worship.

It is because the Liturgical Movement emphasizes the necessity for the whole people to be caught up in the whole offering of worship that we are driven back again on this nagging question of the relation between God and His world. Supposing we make a tentatively fresh start at outlining that relation? Suppose we start by affirming boldly that this is God's world anyway, not a world from which He is in any sense aloof, but one through which His purposes and plans run like the basic framework in a building, one in which His Spirit courses with irrepressible vitality? Suppose we affirm this without any naivety or sentimentality whatever, because whilst we hold that all creation has been infected by the mystery of sin and evil we also hold that the primary fact about the world is that it is God's, willed

11

into being by Him with his order running right through it all and His overwhelming mercy now made plain by the great fact of Christ? Suppose we look to the world's state and to the freshness of contemporary history to show us what God in Christ is now doing?

To look to the contemporary world in order to find the setting for Christ's work enables us to rescue worship from the antiquarian and to use the Bible realistically. The Biblical revelation is given to us so that we can interpret the work and purpose of God correctly. The mighty fact of the Christ-event provides us with the criteria with which to grasp the work which Christ is now continuing to do with modern man. We can now look at the world in the right sort of way, asking the right questions about it and discovering the most significant things about it—because of Christ. We now know Him to be where God's good news is being offered to the poor and despairing and underprivileged; where release is being proclaimed to every sort of prisoner, healing and new sight being granted to every sort of blind man; where every broken, battered victim is being made free and whole again; where the Lord's favour towards mankind is being made patent in new life. Christian worship is not therefore an earnest attempt to get a whole group of twentieth century men to imagine that they are living in Palestine in the first century, and to struggle to get them to use all the imagery and thought-forms of Jews or Greeks. It is an attempt to illuminate and interpret modern life with the permanent and ultimate truth that happened to be made plain in Palestine long ago. It is not therefore an offering of the past, nor a concentration upon the past. It is an offering of the present and a concentration upon the present and future, using a perspective and insight given by the past.

This means that modern Christian cannot escape a basic demythologizing of the Bible in his worship. Nowadays people have very good reason for *not* believing that God tells travellers where to find a baby by moving a star around the heavens and hovering it close over a particular roof. They have good reason for *not* believing that a mental disorder is due to swarms of demons who can be persuaded to jump into a herd of pigs. They have good reason for *not* anticipating tongues of fire to dance over their heads when a group of Christians is inspired and gripped by the Holy Spirit. But if we use the Bible to enable us to *interpret* God's activity today, and not to *determine* how we are to think we rescue Christian worship from an exercise in 'living in the past' and enable it to become an exercise in 'living in the present'. It is precisely because many of the noblest hymns still sung with vigour by Christians are reproductions of how Christian man used to think (but does no longer), that they are becoming an increasing embarrassment today. We urgently need hymns and songs that do not require a great feat of mental transposition before they can be sung wholeheartedly—but we need hymns that sing of the great acts of God going on all around us and within us, for it is in this exciting modern world that God's life and Christ's work are the major matters for Christian rejoicing.

The moment we are in earnest about this, and not merely prepared to kill this primal Biblical insight with some weak slogan like 'religion is concerned with the whole of life', the beginnings of a genuine renewal become possible. But the enormous inertia of our religious past hangs like a millstone about our necks. 'We are heirs of a long period in which all the aspects of the spiritual and also the aesthetic life have been shunted off on to a sidetrack; assigned to a special compartment; banished from the market-place and the crude realities of life; put upon a pedestal or relegated to a shrine.'[1] As a result we have an embarrassed distaste for many of the crucial issues with which men must wrestle (when did you last hear a sermon on 'Is it right to strike?' or 'Is family planning permissible?') and a chronic fear of anything that is controversial and might 'upset some people'. More seriously, we have expected the Word of God to operate either in the secret place of the individual's conscience or in occasional flashes of insight when some word of Scripture or sermon is being spoken to us—whereas the Word lays hold on Christian man in the turmoil of his normal existence, struggling to be true to God in a complex and challenging world, just as it spoke with Saul whilst he was *on the march* with the soldiers. We have presumed that the Holy Spirit comes down to us in individual experiences of beatific emotional release, or sublime ecstasy, and that (to put it crudely) He makes us 'feel grand'—whereas the most powerful work of the Spirit is in equipping the company of Christian people to pursue their immediate tasks with integrity, courage, patience, love. We see Jesus in terms of the gentle white man with beautifully waved hair and deep blue eyes, gathering all the children benignly on to His knee and stroking their locks, like the atrociously sentimental and false pictures that feature in almost every Sunday School in the land (it is salutary to remember that this feature of Jesus' life occupies eight verses in, for example, the whole of Matthew. About two hundred times as much space is taken up with His final judgement of all men and the basis upon which it works! His repudiation of current 'religion' involves about half the whole gospel . . .). So we tame Jesus Christ and relegate Him to the genteel world of tranquil religious contentment, and would be amazed if anyone were seriously to suggest that we find Him in the Trade Union leader battling against genuine injustice, the Freedom Fighter in the United States, the politician in new Africa struggling desperately to retain his integrity,

[1]Amos Wilder, *Other Worldliness and the New Testament*, SCM Press (1965), p.23.

the refugee by the Jordan, the doctor in North Vietnam.

The contributions which we have chosen in this book have been selected because we believe that they represent genuine attempts to break out of sterile patterns and to experiment freely with forms that may enable worship to come alive for contemporary Christians. They are not perfect. Sometimes they appear clumsy, mis-shaped, slick or pompous. Sometimes they require a liturgical sophistication which is lacking in many congregations, who cannot yet bear to have a printed order made available to them, with prayers that have been written out beforehand and require participation through set responses. Sometimes they involve drama or folk music or pageantry in ways that appear alien to the normal Sunday routine. Sometimes they don't quite 'come off'. So they are not printed here to be slavishly copied (although anyone can reproduce any of these acts of worship if he so wishes). They are printed here as illustrations of ways in which various people are trying to renew their worship, and are using genuine insight into the contemporary situation. That is, they have attempted to involve the whole people of God, they have been imaginative, they have believed in a God who meets us in the ordinary life of the modern world and calls us into that life with renewed energy and competence and grace in Christ; they have challenged as well as healed, they have involved new discipleship as well as forgiveness. They have not been remote exercises in spirituality which may just as well have been concocted for people living on the moon in A.D. 300, but the appropriate offering of contemporary man in his glad celebration of the gospel, by which he must live day by day.

Their imperfections are real, and we have added a critique at the end of each act of worship. We have asked members of the Faith and Order Committee of the Methodist Church to add their judgements, and are grateful for this contribution to our work from those appointed by the Methodist Conference to watch over the worship of Methodists. But although this work has a Methodist origin, we have sifted information from many sources and, indeed, many countries. We are profoundly grateful to these many people from many different Church traditions who have sent us material, comment, and encouragement. We hope that the book will be valuable to all Christians everywhere.

God, who sits on the throne, says:

'BEHOLD! I AM MAKING ALL THINGS NEW.'

A NOTE CONCERNING THE BOOK

The Renewal Group approached the Local Preachers Department in 1966 with a view to collaboration over a book of contemporary worship, and proposed three of its members to work on the project. The Department nominated two of its Committee members to work with them. Letters were then sent out to the religious press asking for information on forms of worship and experiments being undertaken throughout the Church. There was a considerable response, and the five members of the group undertook responsibility to evaluate the material and decide which was the most useful for publication. We divided the work in this way:

Orders of Holy Communion and	
Orders for regular morning or evening worship	Trevor Rowe
Family Worship	Wallace White
The Christian Festivals	Brian Frost
Special Themes and Occasions and	
Youth Services	James Bates
Editorial work	Richard Jones

We then formulated our own comments upon those acts of worship which seemed the most significant, and these are printed after each order we have selected. We then sent our material to three members nominated from the Faith and Order Committee—the Revs. Rupert Davies, Raymond George, and Gordon Wakefield—and asked for their comments. These are printed as 'Further comments' after each of the orders chosen.

Normally the hymn numbers refer to the *Methodist Hymn Book* unless otherwise stated (as in order 5.G.). Where abbreviations are used, M is for Minister and P is for People, but in some orders C is preferred for Congregation (as in 1.C.)., or the Minister becomes the Leader, denoted by L. Order 6.B. uses Versicle (V) and Response (R).

ACKNOWLEDGEMENTS

The compilers wish to thank the Renewal Group, the Local Preachers Department, and the Faith and Order Committee, for help and encouragement; the S.C.M. Press and the Architectural Press for permission to quote extracts from books published by them; *New Directions* for an order originally published by them, likewise Christian Aid; Miss Gladys Charlton and Miss Muriel Fletcher for generous help in the typing.

1. Holy Communion

A PRELIMINARY COMMENT
Raymond George

I AM GRATEFUL for the opportunity of reading these experimental forms of worship and commenting on them. Though I was nominated for this purpose, with two others, by the Faith and Order Committee, I write in my own name only; the Committee is in no way responsible for my views. In many cases I endorse the comments already made by the editors and am silent about particular points because they have already been well made.

The Holy Communion raises a special question of authority. The Methodist Church authorizes two orders in the Book of Offices and, though Methodism has never insisted on a rigid uniformity, these orders must be respected as the authorized norm until further action is taken. Many will think that this does not preclude a measure of experiment on appropriate occasions, and from this I do not dissent. However, the Conference of 1968 will probably be presented by the Faith and Order Committee with a new order which it will be asked to authorize for experimental use for three years. This order seeks to embody some of the insights found in other experimental orders which have been circulating. If it is approved it will have an authority which these other orders lack and, though further experiment will not be precluded, it will itself be a kind of norm on which interest should be concentrated.

Thus the publication of these orders does not give them any authority, nor does the co-operation of individual members of the Faith and Order Committee alter that situation in any way. They are published primarily for the purposes of discussion.

ORDERS FOR HOLY COMMUNION

In recent years a number of official or unofficial revisions of Communion Services have appeared. These include: *The Church of South India: The Book of Common Worship* (Oxford, 1963); Cope, Davies, and Tytler: *An Experimental Liturgy* (Lutterworth, Ecumenical Studies in Worship, No. 3, 1958); *The Eucharistic Liturgy of Taizé* (Faith Press, 1962); The Renewal Group: 'An Order of Holy Communion 1962' (printed in *Expository Times*, August, 1965); The

17

Church of England Liturgical Commission: *Alternative Services, Second Series* (SPCK, 1966).

Probably more significant is the fact that within Methodism many people, having found the authorized service in the Book of Offices difficult to use, have taken the law into their own hands and produced their own revisions. Examples of these that have reached us indicate that often enthusiasm has not been matched by understanding. The services printed here *and* our comments upon them may indicate the way Communion Services can be written or adapted for a variety of occasions.

A. THE RENEWAL GROUP'S DRAFT ORDER

This is a revision undertaken by some members of the Renewal Group in a private capacity—not on behalf of the Group. Note: Some of the prayers and responses are intended as examples rather than invariable forms. They are printed without alternative for the sake of clarity.

CONFESSION: BEFORE THE EUCHARIST

M: Our help is in the name of the Lord

P: Who made the heaven and the earth.

M: Let us recall the words of Jesus:
Jesus said, 'You must be perfect even as your Father in heaven is perfect.'

P: Jesus also said, 'I came not to call the righteous but sinners to make a new start.'

MP: Lord, your words disturb us and restore us. If our prayers make us hypocrites, if our money distorts our lives, if our anxiety stops us being free to live, you know our condition and you can heal us. Make us honest with ourselves, yet deliver us from despair. Giver of life and hope we come to you neither to plead nor to boast, but as we are. Accept us, we pray.

SILENCE

M: Jesus says 'You are free. . . . .'

P: O God we praise you,
We acknowledge you to be the Lord.

HYMN 69

18

THE MINISTRY OF THE WORD
(It may be convenient to collect gifts of money by means of a plate at the door, near which stand the bread and wine for the eucharist)
The minister brings the Bible to the table. The people stand.

M: O give thanks to the Lord, for He is good;
His steadfast love endures for ever!
Let the people of God say,
P: His love endures for ever!

M: Let the servants of Christ say,
P: His love endures for ever!

M: Let those who fear the Lord say,
P: His love endures for ever!

THE GLORIA (sung) or HYMN

PRAYER before the Word, e.g. Collect

OLD TESTAMENT LESSON

P: Thanks be to God.

HYMN or PSALM

NEW TESTAMENT LESSON

P: Praise be to Christ, the Living Word.

SERMON

THE APOSTLES' CREED (or the Nicene Creed). All stand.

M: Let us confess our common faith.

THE NOTICES

PRAYERS FOR THE CHURCH AND THE WORLD
(This can vary widely according to local conditions. Members of the congregation may mention particular concerns and the leader (L) proceed with the biddings *or* names may be mentioned during the prayer itself in between each bidding and the response).

L: You know our needs, O Lord, before we ask; but you have called us to pray and so we remember before you our fellows and ourselves. Make us open and ready to translate our words into deeds. We pray for our Queen and political leaders.

L: The Lord hears our prayer.
P: Thanks be to God. We pray for men at war and divided against each other.

L: The Lord hears our prayer.
P: Thanks be to God. We pray for the suffering, the satisfied, and the successful.

L: The Lord hears our prayer.
P: Thanks be to God. We pray for our town.

L: The Lord hears our prayer.
P: Thanks be to God. We pray for our Church, here and in every place.

L: The Lord hears our prayer.
P: Thanks be to God. We pray for your world.

L: The Lord hears our prayer.
P: Thanks be to God.

MP: To your name, O Lord, be glory, praise and worship, now and always. Amen.

THE BREAKING OF BREAD

M: We meet in the name of the risen Lord and the power of his spirit to break bread together. Recalling that God did not spare his own Son, but surrendered him for us all, let us, with these offerings, give our very selves to him, a living sacrifice, dedicated and fit for his acceptance. Freely we have received, let us freely give.

THE OFFERTORY: Bread, Wine, and Money (previously collected) are brought to the table by members of the congregation.

THE EUCHARIST PRAYER

M: The Lord be with you.
P: And with your spirit.

M: Lift up your hearts.
P: We lift them up unto the Lord.

M: Let us give thanks unto the Lord our God.
P: It is meet and right so to do.

M: Let us pray;
It is truly meet and right, our joy and our salvation at all times and in every place to give thanks to You, O Lord, Holy Father, Almighty Everlasting God, through Your beloved Son, Jesus Christ our Lord. For whom and by whom all things exist, Through whom You made the heavens and the earth and man in Your image; who was made man and suffered death upon the cross for our redemption that we, being delivered from the bondage of our rebellion might be Your people, a royal priesthood and a holy nation, to Your praise and glory. Who in the same night that he was betrayed took bread, and after giving thanks broke it and gave it to his

disciples, saying, Take, eat, this is my body which is given for you. In the same way after supper he took the cup and, when He had given thanks, He gave it to them saying, Drink, all of you, of this, for this cup is the new covenant in my blood which is shed for you and for many for the forgiveness of sins;

MP: Amen. Your death, O Lord, we commemorate. Your resurrection we confess, and Your final coming we await.

M: And so, O Father, recalling the precious death and passion, the glorious resurrection and ascension of Your Son our Lord, we Your servants and Your holy people, offer our sacrifice of praise and thanksgiving, with this bread and in this cup that we may be sharers in His body and blood, and receiving the forgiveness of our sins may be filled with the Holy Spirit and grow up in all things into Him who is our Head.

We ask You to accept our prayers and praises before Your Throne on high through Your dear Son, our great High Priest and Mediator, as with all the company of heaven we praise You now and evermore, saying,

MP: Holy, Holy, Holy, Lord God of Hosts,
Heaven and earth are full of Your Glory
Glory be to You, O Lord most high. Amen.

THE FRACTION

(As he says the words the minister breaks the bread and takes the cup.)

M: The bread which we break is the communion of the Body of Christ.

The cup of blessing for which we give thanks is the communion of the blood of Christ.

We who are many are one bread, one body; for we all share the one bread.

THE PEACE

M: If anyone says, I love God, and hates his brother, he is a liar.

P: He who does not love his brother whom he has seen, cannot love God whom he has not seen.

(Here, when it is desired, the Peace may be passed through the congregation, the minister giving the right hand of fellowship to the person nearest to him, and he to his neighbour, and so through the whole company.)

M: The peace of the Lord be always with you.

P: And with your spirit.

THE INVITATION (*All kneel or sit*)

MP: I will receive the Bread of heaven and call upon the name of the Lord; Lord I am not worthy that You should come under my roof, but speak the word only and I shall be healed. May the body of our Lord Jesus Christ preserve my life unto eternity.

What shall I render to the Lord for all His goodness? I will take the cup of salvation and call upon the name of the Lord. May the blood of our Lord Jesus Christ preserve my life unto eternity. Amen

The Minister receives the Communion and then says:

M: Come, for all things are now ready.

THE COMMUNION

(The Distribution will vary according to circumstances. Laymen may assist in the administration of the bread and wine. A suitable hymn or psalm may be sung.)

WORDS OF ADMINISTRATION

(These may be repeated or said once, after which the administration proceeds in silence.)

M: The Body of our Lord Jesus Christ, which was given for you, preserve you unto everlasting life. Take and eat this in remembrance that Christ died for you, and feed on Him in your heart by faith with thanksgiving.

The Blood of our Lord Jesus Christ, which was shed for you, preserve you unto everlasting life. Drink this in remembrance that Christ's Blood was shed for you, and be thankful.

After the Communion the minister says:

M: And now as our Lord has taught us we dare to say,

MP: Our Father, who art in heaven, Hallowed be Thy Name. Thy kingdom come. Thy will be done, on earth, as it is in heaven. Give us this day our daily bread. And forgive us our trespasses, As we forgive those who trespass against us. And lead us not into temptation; But deliver us from evil: For Thine is the kingdom, The power, and the glory, For ever and ever. Amen.

M: Finished and perfected, O Christ our God, as far as in us lies, is the mystery which You have ordained. We have made the memorial of Your death. We have seen the symbol of Your resurrection; we have been filled through Your unfailing goodness, and made rich with Your undying life. In thankfulness we offer You our life for the sake of the world. May Your body, the Church, be broken never by the pride and divisions of Your people, but only in the way of the cross. Spirit of the Lord, so be upon the Church that in and through her life our Saviour Jesus Christ may preach good news to the poor, proclaim release to the captives, and recovering of sight to the blind, set at liberty those who are oppressed, and proclaim the acceptable year of the Lord. Amen.

THE DISMISSAL

M: Go forth into the world in peace; be of good courage, hold fast to that which is good; render to no man evil for evil; strengthen the faint hearted; support the weak, help the afflicted; honour all men; love and serve the Lord, rejoicing in the power of the Holy Spirit. And the blessing of God Almighty, the Father, the Son, and the Holy Spirit, be upon you, and remain with you for ever.

P: Amen.

Comments

1. The parts of the service are set out well and the order of the service is basically right. The placing of, say, the Creed and The Lord's Prayer are matters of debate and are not very important compared with the 'flow' of the service. The Confession is made to be what it ought to be: a prologue external to the main two-part shape of the service. The two parts (The Ministry of the Word; The Breaking of Bread) are indicated not just by headings in the printed order, but by the action of the minister in bringing the Bible to the table, and the Bread, Wine, and Money being brought to the table by members of the congregation.

2. The language has freshness, but many will object to its 'two languages'. It does not make up its mind whether to be contemporary or not. Thus the unity of the service is undermined. Those who write communion orders must decide what liturgical elements are needed and then write them up in one style. But it must be remembered that, for example, the prayer of Confession printed is not intended as an invariable form. This sort of language may lose its freshness quickly and new forms would have to develop.

3. The sequence of subjects in 'Prayers for the Church and the World' is not easy to understand. A more natural order would be: for your world, for your Church, for our Queen, for our town, for men at war ..., for the suffering. ... This would not be ideal, but would be closer to the principle for shaping intercession: set the total content out in two opening petitions—pray for the salvation of the world and for the Church that bears a ministry of reconciliation

23

to the world; then break this down in the following petitions—praying for international, national, and community needs; then for the suffering, and finally for the congregation and those who are part of it.

4. The order lacks provision for well-chosen hymns at key points in the service, as if hymn-singing was an embarrassment to the compilers. A hymn such as 114 (but not all verses), 243, or 251 would make a more exultant vehicle of praise than the prayer following the Lord's Prayer after Communion.

5. The Peace is an action that many find intensely moving and others find embarrassing. It would be useful for groups who have experienced this action to explore together the reasons for these two reactions. Much hand-shaking does occur within Methodism, and it does not seem inappropriate to give it a liturgical setting. In view of the diversity of welcome given to this practice, the order seems right in making it an optional extra.

Further Comments

1. The problem raised above of the two 'languages' is difficult. For some time to come we must be content with a mixture. We do not yet have a satisfactory modern version of the Lord's Prayer, and many hymns worth preserving cannot be modernized. Moreover, if there are to be two styles it seems appropriate that the confession and intercessions should go furthest in the modern style, even if here the clash seems jarring. The more ephemeral and garish colloquialisms have certainly been avoided.

2. A more direct scriptural word of absolution might be better, and hymn 69 is not set to a good enough tune to be appropriate at this stage.

3. This group was clearly well-informed on liturgical matters. The order follows the widely-held theory that the Sanctus ('Holy, holy, holy . . .') stood originally at the close of the eucharistic prayer, but this theory has not won universal approval.

4. The question at which point we should express our self-oblation is very complex. This service has not made up its mind. It almost does it twice—once before the offertory ('let us with these offerings give our very selves . . .') and again in the eucharistic prayer ('we . . . offer our sacrifice of praise . . .'). The offering of ourselves and our praise cannot easily be separated in this way.

5. Why in the intercessions should it be 'our town' and 'our Church' but 'your world'?

6. Apart from one reference to the 'company of heaven' there is no commemoration of the departed.

7. It seems mistaken to put 'let us pray' between 'It is meet and right so to do' and 'It is truly meet and right.'

8. Many modern liturgies have the Pauline sentence about the cup at the Fraction, but since the Fraction concerns the bread alone this seems unnecessary.

9. It is good to have the Peace and there is precedent for having it at this point, but it breaks the four-action shape (He took . . . blessed . . . broke . . . gave). It might be preferable at the beginning of the Ministry of the Sacrament, since there is a danger of interposing too much between the Great Prayer and the Distribution.

10. The Lord's Prayer is usually now put earlier, although this traditional Anglican-Methodist position still has a few defenders. After all, at this point we can say 'Our Father' at a different level of conviction than before.

11. This form of dismissal is popular, but seems likely to produce a jumbled effect in the mind.

B. SHORT MID-WEEK ORDER

Source: Rev. James Bates

THE INVOCATION

M: Behold the dwelling of God is with men.
       He will dwell with them
       And they shall be His people
       And God himself shall be with them.
       Our Help is in the name of the Lord
       Who made heaven and earth.

THE CONFESSION

MP: We confess to God the Father
       That we have sinned in thought, word and deed;
       We have not loved Him with all our being
       We have not cared for others as for ourselves.

M: The Lord hears us and forgives us,
       Delivers us from all wrong,
       And strengthens us in all goodness.
       In His great love he accepts us,
       And makes us his.

P: Thanks be to God. Amen.

THE LESSON

THE INTERCESSION

M: Let us pray to God the Father
For the Church of Jesus Christ in all the world
That it may live in unity and love;
For the peace of the world, and the well-being of all men
That they may find joy and freedom in Christ;
For all those in distress,
That they may be delivered, and find strength in time of need;
For this college and all who work here
That we may serve God faithfully and as one family.

M: The Lord hears our prayer.
P: Thanks be to God.

THE OFFERING AND THANKSGIVING

M: Blessed be God our Father for the bread of the earth,
    For food and shelter,
    For the toil and skill of man,
    For our common life together,
    For Christ, the bread of life.
Blessed be God our Father for the fruit of the vine,
    For the joy and gladness of this life,
    For human care and love,
    For the gift of Christ His Son,
    And his sacrifice for us.

MP: Holy, Holy, Holy,
Lord God of hosts,
Heaven and earth are full of Thy glory.

M: Blessed is he that comes in the name of the Lord.
P: Hosanna in the highest.

THE HYMN

THE INSTITUTION

M: The Lord Jesus, in the same night that he was betrayed, took bread and, when he had given thanks, brake it and gave it to his disciples, saying, Take, eat, This is my body which is given for you:
Do this in remembrance of me.
Likewise after supper he took the cup and, when he had given thanks he gave it to his disciples, saying: Drink ye all of this for this cup is the new covenant in my blood which is shed for you and for many for the remission of sins: whenever ye drink it, do this in remembrance of me.

MP: Whenever we eat this bread and drink this cup, we proclaim the Lord's death 'till he come.

26

THE COMMUNION

THE CONCLUSION

M: O Lord, by the love of Christ, we are thine.

P: Take us and use us as thy people.

M: The whole earth is thine.

P: Here let us work to thy glory.

MP: Our Father. . . .

THE BLESSING

Comments

1. This service was designed to provide a Communion order for an occasion when brevity was essential. It indicates how an order can be adapted to fit an occasion without damaging the basic structure of the service. The preparation in the form of 'The Invocation' and 'The Confession' is brief and to the point. The Service of the Word has traditionally three essentials: reading from the Bible, Sermon, and Intercessions. Here the Sermon is missing. It is a pity that this should be the victim of brevity. A sermon need not be twenty minutes in length. It could take the form of half a dozen sentences relating the lesson read to the situation of the congregation. Radio and TV have shown how four minutes can be used very effectively.

2. Unless it was very carefully chosen, the Hymn, in the middle of what amounts to 'The Great Prayer of Thanksgiving', could be disastrous. It hardly seems necessary here and could also be excluded in the interests of both brevity and good liturgy. But hymns 89, 92, 95, 96 (2 verses), 115, 114 (some verses), 243, and 249 might be considered for use at this point.

3. There is no indication that the people take any part in the offertory. The action of giving identifies the people with the bread and wine more than any form of words can do.

Further Comments

1. The Great Prayer of Thanksgiving leaves out essential items. To the portion about the bread and wine it adds a mere three lines about Christ. This is no adequate substitute for recalling his death, resurrection, ascension, and heavenly session, and for referring to the Holy Spirit. That is, it lacks an Anamnesis and an Epiclesis. If it be said that these are not needed because 'consecration is by thanksgiving', it must still be noted that this thanksgiving is too meagre.

2. Like 1662 and kindred rites there is nothing which corresponds to an oblation of ourselves.

3. It is not clear whether the words of Institution are being read 'as a warrant' or whether they are accidentally cut off from the prayer in which they are usually incorporated. It is quite wrong to have the hymn before them.

Writing the Congregation's Own Liturgy
If a group of people sit down to write an order of service for their own local situation they are unlikely to produce an 'immortal' liturgy—for there is no such thing! But they will have something that is *theirs*—words they can speak honestly and things they can do with understanding. Here in the next three examples are the results of groups of people doing this.

C. THE EUCHARISTIC LITURGY

As prepared by the People and Clergy of St. Mark's-in-the-Bowerie, New York, for use on special Ecumenical Occasions.

THE PREPARATION
At the appointed time, when all the people have assembled, the president of the assembly, shall say:

P(resident)   We are here

A(ssembly):   In the name of Jesus Christ.

P and A: We are here because we are men—but we deny our humanity. We are stubborn fools and liars to ourselves. We do not love others. We war against life. We hurt each other. We are sorry for it and know we are sick from it. We seek new life.

P: Giver of life, heal us and free us to be men.

P and A: Holy Spirit speak to us. Help us to listen for we are very deaf. Come, fill this moment.

Silence for a time

THE SERVICE OF THE WORD
OLD TESTAMENT LESSON

PSALM   (*said responsively*)

EPISTLE   (Read from the same place and in like manner to Old Testament Lesson)

HYMN

THE GOSPEL   (Read in the midst of the assembly, all the people facing the reader)

SERMON

(The deacon shall bid the prayers and intercessions of the assembly. He may lead them in a litany or with free prayers)

THE OFFERTORY

The president shall begin the offertory with the following words:

> If, when you are bringing your gift to the altar, you suddenly remember that your brother has a grievance against you, leave your gift where it is before the altar. First go and make your peace with your brother, and only then come back and offer your gift. (Matt. 5: 23).

After which he will turn to the deacon first and then the reader saying:

> Peace, my friend.

And the deacon will answer:

> Peace.

Then the deacon and reader will give the 'Peace' to representatives of the congregation gathered before the altar table, and they in turn will pass it to all the people, while others will collect the alms
Then the president shall read the following words:

> Therefore, my brothers, I implore you by God's mercy to offer your very selves to him: a living sacrifice, dedicated and fit for his acceptance, the worship offered by mind and heart. Adapt yourselves no longer to the pattern of this present world, but let your minds be remade and your whole nature thus transformed. Then you will be able to discern the will of God, and to know what is good, acceptable and perfect. (Romans 12: 1-2)

Then shall be sung a hymn, during which time the representatives of the people will bring the money along with bread, water and wine, and place them on the holy table. The deacon shall prepare the bread and wine.

THE ACT OF THANKSGIVING

P: Lift up your hearts.
A: We lift them to the Lord.

P: Let us give thanks for God's glory.
A: We give thanks, we rejoice in the glory of all creation.

P: All glory be to you, O Father, who sent your only son into the world to be a man, born of a woman's womb, to die for us on a cross that was made by us.
A: He came for us. Help us to accept his coming.

P: He walked among us, a man, on our earth, in our world of conflict, and commanded us to remember his death, his death which gives us life; and to wait for him until he comes again in glory.

A: We remember his death; we live by his presence; we wait for his coming.

P: On the night he was betrayed, the Lord Jesus took bread (*Here he should lift up the bread in thanksgiving*), he gave thanks; he broke it, and gave it to his disciples, saying, 'Take, eat, this is my body. Do this in remembrance of me.' He also took the cup (*and here he should lift up the wine*); he gave thanks; and gave it to them, saying, 'Drink of it, all of you; this is my blood of the covenant, which is poured out for many for the forgiveness of sins.'

A: Come, Lord Jesus, come.

P: Therefore, remembering his death, believing in his rising from the grave, longing to recognize his presence; now, in this place, we obey his command; we offer bread and wine, we offer ourselves, to be used.

A: Everything is yours, O Lord; we return the gift which first you gave us.

P: Accept it, Father. Send down the spirit of life and power, glory and love, upon these people, upon this bread and wine (*Here he may extend his hands over the bread and wine*), that to us they may be his body and his blood.

A: Come, risen Lord, live in us that we may live in you.

P: Now with all men who ever were, are, and will be, with all creation in all time, with joy we sing (*or say*):

P&A: Holy, Holy, Holy, Lord God Almighty, all space and all time show forth your glory now and always. Amen.

P: And now, in his words, we are bold to say:
Our Father . . .

Then shall the president break the bread before the assembly, saying:

P: The gifts of God for the people of God
A: Amen

THE COMMUNION

Then shall the president and other ministers receive Holy Communion into their hands, and then distribute the bread and wine to all present. For the bread shall be said:

P: The Body of Christ.
A: Amen.

For the wine shall be said:
P: The Blood of Christ.
A: Amen.
HYMN
THE DISMISSAL
P: Go. Serve the Lord. You are free.
A: Amen.

Comments

1. This order we regard as excellent—a real, modern Communion order, liturgically accurate, with an active place for the people and a distinct healthiness about the language—it is appropriate language, fresh and understandable, yet never banal or trivial. All this is particularly seen in the Great Prayer of Thanksgiving which has been devised to give the people a full part, and to flow along simply and steadily without any waste of words or long pauses.

2. The two actions around which ritual developed early on in the Church's history were the reading of the Gospel and the Offertory. The collection in a Methodist preaching service is almost the only piece of ritual to be found in it. An Offertory procession at Holy Communion would seem to be a natural development of this. In this order the reading of the Gospel is given a special place by being read from 'the midst of the assembly'. This is one of those pieces of ritual—like 'the Peace' that don't look very impressive on paper but are powerful and moving in action.

3. This order is marked by extreme brevity after the act of Communion. The temptation is to linger on in pious meditation. This order calls us to act out in the world what we have acted out in church.

Further Comments

1. This is certainly a liturgy in the classic shape, as is clear in the Act of Thanksgiving whose composition was obviously guided by skilled liturgists. It embodies that view of the Sanctus discussed earlier under the Renewal Group's order.

2. The interesting novelties are the large number of responses by the people in the Act of Thanksgiving and the modern style of the language, which reaches its peak in the confession.

3. The order lacks a commemoration of the departed. The Offertory is superb, but there is a danger of exaggerating this element in the Eucharist. The phrase 'a woman's womb' jars slightly.

4. The opening words 'we are here' would be a little unfortunate in congregations aware of a certain camp fire song. . . . It would be preferable for the president to say 'we are here in the name of Jesus Christ'.

D. A SERVICE OF HOLY COMMUNION FOR STUDENTS

Source: Southampton University Free Church Society

A HYMN

A PASSAGE OF SCRIPTURE

Prayer of Confession through comparison with Jesus Christ

M: Let us examine ourselves in the light of Jesus Christ
Let us pray:
Our Father, God, as we look at the life, death and resurrection of Your Son, we see in ourselves many weaknesses and failings.
Christ was patient, ready and willing to talk with, and listen to anyone and everyone. He said 'Let the children come unto me', even when his disciples considered him far too busy to concern himself with children. So often we are impatient, we don't listen to those whom we dislike.

P: Lord, forgive our impatience, teach us to be patient.

M: Christ mixed with, and served all people. To him sickness was to be healed whoever needed healing. Too frequently we meet only with people of our own type, we are selective as to those we talk with, and those we help.

P: Lord, forgive us, help us to be a friend to all.

M: Christ was unselfish in all things, even to the extent of forgetting family and friends, even to giving himself. We can give where we can expect to receive: we can give when it doesn't hurt.

P: Lord, forgive our selfishness, teach us to be unselfish.

M: Christ was always constant, he lived as he preached. Too often our words are not reflected in our actions.

P: Lord, forgive us, strengthen us that we may act as we speak.

M: Jesus Christ was forgiving; even as he died he said 'Forgive them Father!' We so often harbour a grudge, unwilling to forgive.

P: Lord, forgive us our trespasses, and teach us to forgive those who trespass against us.

M: Christ suffered and died on the cross for our sins.

P: Lord, we admit that often we are afraid to suffer the scorn of men for your sake; forgive us, give us courage that we may be bold in your name. Amen.

M: O God, we acknowledge that we have committed many sins, some which we can see, many which we cannot see ourselves. We have followed our own desires, and have neglected to obey your laws. We have done things which we know to be wrong in your eyes, and have failed to serve you in many things. We ask, O Lord, your forgiveness through Jesus Christ; teach us by our mistakes and grant us strength not to fail in the same way again. We ask this in Christ's name. Amen.

St. John says this: If we claim to be sinless, we are self-deceived and strangers to the truth. If we confess our sins he is just, and may be trusted to forgive our sins and to cleanse us from every kind of wrong. (1 John 1: 8, 9.)

A HYMN

A LESSON

SERMON

PRAYER OF INTERCESSION

M: For the salvation of mankind and the peace of the whole world let us pray to the Lord.

P: Bless us, O Lord, for your mercy's sake.

M: For the whole Church, for its faith and unity and for its constant renewal by the Holy Spirit.

P: Bless us, O Lord, for your mercy's sake.

M: For all nations and governments, that they may impartially seek justice and freedom for all men, let us pray to the Lord.

P: Bless us, O Lord, for your mercy's sake.

M: For our country, for our Parliament and Prime Minister, for Elizabeth our Queen, and for all her subjects, that they may diligently and faithfully seek the common good, let us pray to the Lord.

P: Bless us, O Lord, for your mercy's sake.

M: For this modern age, that men may rejoice in the gifts of creation and in the work of their hands, using them with reverence and for good ends, let us pray to the Lord.

P: Bless us, O Lord, for your mercy's sake.

M: For all in need, sorrow and sickness, all who suffer from the cruelty, violence, or neglect of others, especially the very young and the aged, let us pray to the Lord.

P: Bless us, O Lord, for your mercy's sake.

M: For the communion of saints in heaven and on earth, for all souls departed, and that we may be made worthy to join our friends above and share with them in eternal joy.

P: Bless us, O Lord, for your mercy's sake. Amen.

HYMN

The congregation will remain standing

AFFIRMATION OF THE FAITH

P: We believe in one God, the Father, the creator of all things. We believe in Jesus Christ, the only Son of God, born into this world; who was crucified for us, who rose from the dead and ascended to the Father, and against whose example we shall be judged.

We believe in the Holy Spirit, who is the Father and the Son present and active in the world at all times.

We believe in the forgiveness of sins through Jesus Christ and in the life eternal.

We believe in one Church, the body of Christ.

THE INSTITUTION OF THE LORD'S SUPPER (1 Corinthians 11:23-26).

M: The Lord Jesus, on the night of his arrest, took bread and, after giving thanks to God, broke it and said: 'This is my body, which is for you; do this as a memorial of me' In the same way, he took the cup after supper and said: 'This cup is the new covenant sealed by my blood. Whenever you drink it, do this as a memorial of me.' For every time you eat this bread and drink the cup, you proclaim the death of the Lord until he comes.

THE INVITATION

M: You, who do truly and earnestly repent of your sins, and are in love and charity with your neighbours, and intend to lead a new life following the commandments of God, and walking from now on in His holy ways; draw near in faith and take this holy Sacrament to your comfort.

THE BREAKING OF THE BREAD (The minister shall break the bread in the sight of the congregation).

M: The bread which we break, is it not the communion of the body of Christ?

This cup is the new covenant sealed by the blood of Christ.

The congregation will be seated

PRAYER OF ACCESS

P: We realize our unworthiness to approach you, O God, in our own strength, but we come trusting in your strength, love and forgiveness. We ask that through the body and blood of your Son, Jesus Christ, we may be renewed and that we may live in him and he in us, for ever. Amen.

THE ADMINISTRATION

The words of administration: The body of Christ given for you.

The blood of Christ shed for you.

PRAYERS

After all have received the communion, there will be a period for private prayer—of thanksgiving and committal.

Thanks for the privilege and opportunity of receiving this communion and of sharing in Christ.

Remembrance of and thanksgiving for, the life, death, and resurrection of Jesus Christ.

Thanks for our life in Christ now.

M: And now we are bold to say:

P: Our Father, ...

PRAYER OF COMMITTAL

M: O Lord, our heavenly Father, we ask you to accept our offerings of praise and thanksgiving. Grant that by the perfect life and sacrifice of your Son, and through faith in him, we and all believers may be forgiven our sins and obtain full salvation. We surrender to you, our Lord, our bodies and souls, that we may become living instruments of your holy will, and humbly we ask you to bless all who have taken part in this holy Communion, and fill us with your grace. Although through our sinfulness our sacrifice is made unworthy, yet we ask you to accept this our duty and service; and not judging our faults, forgive us our sins

Through the saving power of Jesus Christ our Lord. Amen

HYMN

BENEDICTION

Comments

1. This is not an order we would commend for use. As a 'home-made' it illustrates many of the pitfalls that lie in the way of such an enterprize. The Southampton students are to be commended for their attempt, an honest one in that it indicates many typical student attitudes.

2. The Confession at the beginning is very individualistic. It is good to have the Confession at the beginning so that from that point the congregation can move into the proper joy of celebrating Word and Sacrament, but here one wonders if after the intensity of the Confession this would be possible. Confession, if it is to be more than a personal indulgence, must take into account corporate sin, otherwise an individualism is introduced at the beginning that

militates against the character of the following actions. Even after the large block of confession at the beginning, at two points later on one gets the impression that the authors were not sure that this was enough.

3. A fault that keeps recurring in the orders received is the assumption that all that is needed before communion is to read the account of the Last Supper. This part of the service ought to be an acting over again of the four actions of Jesus at the Supper: taking, blessing, breaking, giving. This order seems to have no offertory (taking) or thanksgiving (blessing).

4. What is the meaning of the response of the congregation in the Prayer of Intercession? Something much simpler and more direct is required.

5. If the Creed is to be said, let it be in ungarbled form. These lowest-common-denominator affirmations of faith offered with a zeal for integrity have a touch of arrogance towards preceding generations.

6. The post-communion prayers are too long and attempt to make up for elements lacking earlier on.

Further Comments

1. Do we want Communion services for special groups of people (such as students), or is it not better to have a definitive order which may be used by specific groups where desired? The Eucharist is the worship of the *Church*, not a select group.

2. The chief weakness is the lack of a Great Prayer of Thanksgiving and Remembrance. Here the heart of the service is not such a thanksgiving with an oblation, but the breaking of the bread. This is a grave deficiency.

E. COMMENTARY ON THE SERVICE IN MODERN ENGLISH

Source: St. Mary's Church, Ware

This is an attempt to take 'A Draft Order for Communion' (The Church of England Liturgical Commission: Alternative Services. Second Series) and write up the prayers in contemporary idiom on a 'commentary page' printed opposite the actual order. We give as an illustration of the endeavour 'The Act of Thanksgiving'.

THE ACT OF THANKSGIVING

M: May you feel the nearness of God.

P: *And so may you too.*

M : Concentrate your thoughts and feelings.

P : *We are focusing them on God.*

M : Let's thank him then.

P : *That's right!*

M : It is surely right to thank you, God of limitless love, our aim, our controller, our father. We thank you for all your loving care for us and all people.

We thank you for creating the universe, and keeping it going. We thank you for all the excitement and delight of the life we live.

But above all we thank you for the infinite love you showed us when the Son lived among us as the man Jesus and won us back to you.

And we thank you for the power of the Holy Spirit in our lives;

And for the promise of life with you after death.

So, along with every intelligent being you have made, we gladly and boldly admit how wonderful you are.

All : *Holy, Holy, Holy, God the source and controller and goal of creation, everything you have made can reflect in some way your love. May everything capable of loving, love you in return.*

M : GOD, you are like a father to us. As the man Jesus, you gave yourself to us in life and in death; and you still give yourself to us in life again. We trust you to use that perfect act of love to draw out from us a perfect love in return.

May we eat the bread and drink the wine as a way of sharing in Jesus' life and death, and as a way of getting a sense of his nearness to us; Just as he told us to.

(The night he was handed over, he took the bread, gave thanks to God over it, and broke it in pieces. He gave it to his friends and said, This is myself. I give myself up to die for you. Do this as a way of sharing my life, and feeling me near to you. In the same way, at the end of the meal, he took the cup, and said thanks to God over that, too. Then he gave it to them, and said, All of you take a drink from it. This is myself. I give myself up to start a new friendship between men and God. I do it for you and for millions more, to bring you all close to God. Do this, whenever you all have a meal together, as a way of sharing my life, and feeling me close to you.)

GOD, you are like a father to us, so we do as Jesus told us to; and we ask you to bring into our lives, here and now, the results of what Jesus did when he died for us, and came alive for us. May we trust the love you showed us in Jesus, and may that love work in us to win us back to you completely.

37

Please accept us and our praise and thanks.
May the whole universe reflect perfectly the love that is your life.

All: *We really mean this.*

Comments

1. Here the liturgical elements have been chosen already by the Draft Order and the author has given us his own reading of them. Such a process inevitably results in both gains and losses. For example, the number of words seems to be greater. Sometimes this has involved using a somewhat clumsy phrase ('May you feel the nearness of God') when the traditional form was much sharper and just as clear ('The Lord be with you'). Again, 'Do this in remembrance' becomes 'Do this as a way of sharing my life, and feeling me near to you'. The constant mention of 'feeling God' has weakened the force of the shorter, sharper phrases. But more serious is the apparent desire to tame down the major assertions of the Christian faith—Christ's resurrection has become 'the promise of life with you after death' and 'you still give yourself to us in life again', whereas his ascension seems to have disappeared altogether.

2. On the other hand many mysterious but traditional phrases have acquired new power and simplicity and meaning—'It is meet and right so to do' has become 'That's right!'; 'angels and archangels and all the company of heaven' have become 'every intelligent being you have ever made'.

3. The over-all impression is that this is a serious attempt to enable a congregation to follow the service and at the same time to have a paraphrase which attempts to interpret the traditional prayers and words which churchmen take for granted. But we doubt whether this has quite 'come off' because the main effect has been to emphasize 'feelings' and to weaken the power of the primary Christian affirmations. To attempt to remove every trace of 'other-worldliness' is bound to result in this weakening.

2. Morning and Evening Worship

EXPERIMENTAL FORMS of worship to cater for the traditional acts of morning and evening worship appear to aim at two goals: the creation of a significant shape to the act of worship; and the involvement of the whole congregation in what is being done.

A. A PATTERN FOR PREACHING SERVICES

Source: Rev. Colin Groom
Note 1. (*) denotes an optional item, and (**) the alternative position of an item which is better placed elsewhere.
2. Sections marked 'L' are spoken by the leader alone; those marked 'P' by the people.
3. Where children attend, the best arrangement is for them to share in section I and III, instead of section II. If this is impracticable, other arrangements can be made.

1. OPENING WORSHIP

(* Choral Introit)
Call to worship (L)
Hymn
Prayer of Adoration and Thanksgiving:
    firstly in the leader's words, and then
    L: Worthy is the Lamb to receive all honour and glory and praise:
    P: Amen! Praise and glory and might be to our God for ever and ever!
Prayer of Invocation, asking God to be present:
    L: Almighty God, Creator, Saviour and Comforter,
    P: Come amongst us, and dwell in our hearts in love, O Lord.
Prayer of Confession, with Mutual Prayer for Forgiveness:
    The Leader firstly makes extempore prayer of confession, and then:
    L: I confess to God Almighty, and to you His People, that I have sinned in my actions, words, and thoughts, and I pray God Almighty to have mercy on me.

P: May the almighty and merciful Lord grant you pardon, time for amendment of life, and the comfort of His Holy Spirit.

L: Amen.

P: We confess to God Almighty, and to His people, that we have sinned in our actions, words, and thoughts, and we pray God Almighty to have mercy on us.

L: May the almighty and merciful Lord grant you pardon, time for amendment of life, and the comfort of His Holy Spirit.

P: Amen.

Hymn

II. THE WORD OF GOD

The Word of God in Lessons and Preaching.

Varying circumstances make several alternatives necessary here, as follows:

Either (a) Old Testament Lesson
(* Choir Anthem)
New Testament Lesson
Hymn
Sermon

Or   (b) Old Testament Lesson
New Testament Lesson
(* Children's Address)
Hymn
(** Offering & Offertory Prayer)
Sermon

Or   (c) Old Testament Lesson
(* Children's Address)
Hymn
(** Offering & Offertory Prayer)
New Testament Lesson
Sermon

Then follows our Response, consisting of two actions, one verbal, the other practical:

A Hymn of Commitment, or the Apostles' Creed, as follows (all stand):

L & P: We commit ourselves to God, the Father Almighty, Maker of this and all worlds; and to Jesus Christ His only Son, our Lord; who was conceived by the Holy Spirit, and born to Mary; He suffered under Pontius Pilate, was crucified, dead, and buried: He descended into hell; on the third day He rose again from the dead; He ascended into heaven; and sits on the right hand of God the Father Almighty; from thence He shall come to judge the living and the dead. We commit ourselves to the Holy Spirit; the holy and universal church; the fellowship of the saints; the forgiveness of sins; the resurrection of the Body of Christ. (1); and the life everlasting. Amen.

(NB (1)—that is, the resurrection of that community which now forms nothing less than the physical presence of Jesus in the world—in short, the Church.)

The Offering, collected, brought to the Holy Table, and dedicated.

III. FINAL PRAYERS AND PRAISES

The Notices

Prayers of Intercession (for others) and Petition (for ourselves). The needs of particular people, and particular needs which we have, will be mentioned. Opportunity will also be given for silent prayer. After each need has been mentioned, and after the silence, this response is said:

L: In Your mercy, O Lord
P: Hear our prayer

The Lord's Prayer, spoken by L & P.
Our Father in heaven, may Your Name be honoured, may Your Kingdom come, and Your will be done on earth as it is in heaven. Give us today the bread we need; forgive us the wrong we have done, as we have forgiven those who have wronged us. Do not expose us to an overwhelming test, but deliver us from the evil one. For Yours is the kingdom, the power, and the glory, for ever. Amen.

(Or the traditional form may be sung.)

Hymn (after which all remain standing.)

Acclamation. Thanks for all Saints Departed, and Exhortation:

L: Praise God for His glorious gospel!
P: Glory be to God for all things!

L: Praise Him for the saints at rest, who await His final victory.
P: They, with united breath, ascribe their conquest to the Lamb.

L: Go back into the world with God: be of good courage; stay true to the gospel; serve the Lord in daily life.

P: We will render to no man evil for evil; we will strengthen the fainthearted and support the weak, and build up the kingdom of love—if God be with us.

The Blessing

L: The blessing of God Almighty, the Father, the Son, and the Holy Spirit, be amongst you and remain with you always.
> (Or another blessing.)

P: Amen.

Comments

1. The pattern of worship ought not to be, 'We are here. God, come and join us,' but 'God is here. May the Spirit help us to realize His presence—making His presence powerful by our openness towards Him.' This the Prayer of Invocation does not quite succeed in doing.

2. The Mutual Prayer for Forgiveness is good in an adult setting; perhaps among children it might raise some interesting questions about the especial sinfulness of the Leader.

3. An interesting use of the Creed is made. While this may be acceptable for occasional use it might be unwise to have a regular practice at odds with the traditional role of the Creed in worship. One important purpose of the Creed used in worship is to introduce a consensus of Christian orthodoxy, free from the inevitable heterodoxy of individuals. Here we have one item individualistically singled out for demythologizing, i.e. the resurrection of the body. The interpretation of this item is clearly different from the intention of the authors of the Creed! Why leave so many other items without demythologizing?

5. When a significant place for the Offertory has been found why are alternative places suggested that lack significance?

5. The mixture of language is difficult. The order would be greatly improved if fresh NEB-style language was employed for everything else and the Creed was deliberately set in traditional style.

6. Must we have even the suggestion that a children's address might be given? If the children are to be present for the sermon let it be a sermon to which all can listen. Surely we cannot any longer give them a sweet (sweet-nothings usually) to keep them quiet through the sermon. This will not do. It lacks in respect for the children.

7. It is an excellent idea to bring the children in for Pt. III. In spite of the difficulties of timing it would be better to have the child-

ren in for this rather than Pt. I when there is an emphasis on confession which is unreal to children in its liturgical and theological setting.

Further Comments

1. The same fate as noted above for the Creed has also afflicted the Lord's Prayer, one phrase having been singled out for an explanatory expansion. The word 'overwhelming' is thus jarring.

2. The Communion Service has a Great Prayer of Thanksgiving for creation and redemption as its climax. This is the best pattern for the preaching service also. In other words, it should be what is sometimes called a 'dry' Eucharist (those who wish to learn more about this view might well study the writings of W. D. Maxwell, although the idea can be found in many other places and goes back, in a sense, to Calvin). The practice of confining the 'long' prayer to intercession is really inherited from the Anglican custom of having intercessions after the third Collect at Morning and Evening Prayer, and we need *not* imitate it. The fundamental reason for putting thanksgiving in the final prayer is that the lessons and sermon expound God's mighty acts in creation and redemption, and evoke our grateful response. Other publications of the Local Preachers Department assume that thanksgiving will go into the first prayer and the same feature occurs elsewhere in this book. The same criticism applies in all such cases.

3. The snippet of a hymn ('they with united breath . . .') does not fit well into a prose context.

4. The over-all impression is of a little too much lecture on worship (albeit good lecture), and some idiosyncrasy. Yet some of the items, having movement in them, are excellent.

B. ORDER FOR SUNDAY EVENING

Source: New Malton Congregational Church
This is a simple layout that gives shape to the service. It is included here for that reason only.

        Announcements (by the Church Secretary)
Approach to God
        Call to worship
        Prayer of Adoration and Invocation
        Hymn
        Prayers of—Confession
                      Assurance of forgiveness
                      Supplication

The Ministry of the Word
> First Reading from the Scriptures
> Anthem or Hymn
> YPF leave during organ voluntary
> Second Reading from the Scriptures
> Anthem or Hymn
> Sermon

Our Response to God's Word
> Hymn
> Offering of Prayer for
>> The Family of the Church
>> For our Friends and
>> For those in Need.
> The Lord's Prayer (said/sung)

Offering of Gifts (Preacher comes down from pulpit to receive gifts)
> Prayer of Dedication
> Hymn
> Benediction (From behind Communion Table)

Comments

1. The subjects for the prayers are oddly worded and their order could be questioned. Do you adore before you invoke or the other way round? What are you supplicating for and why at this point in the service? These questions must be thought out before any person begins to lead public prayer. The intercessory prayer seems to suggest that there is no effort to pray widely for the world.

2. Church announcements could be included before the intercessions so that the activities of the church can be taken up in the prayers. The offering of gifts might also come before the intercessions so that the congregation makes an offering of thanksgiving and prayer together.

3. It is good to see some movement within the service, but it is important that it be significant movement. The congregation must have some idea of why the Benediction is given from behind the Communion Table. Uninterpreted movement in a service has little point—puzzlement is not an adequate replacement for boredom.

Further Comments

1. Presumably supplication means petition (such as a Collect). There is no thanksgiving *at all* here. The intercessions could be somewhat introverted if they always follow this pattern.

2. It is a pity that the YPF should be encouraged to leave early in the service. Evening worship should be such that they may confidently take part in it all.

C. ORDER OF EVENING WORSHIP

Source: Rev. Peter Smith

This service spells out a good shape for an act of worship.

PREPARATION	The Bible is brought in by the Steward, after which silence should be observed for private meditation.
CALL TO WORSHIP	Choir introit or suitable text from the Bible.
HYMN	Praise and Adoration (Our first act of worship is to come before God in Adoration).
PRAYER	Adoration. Confession (Realizing something of God's greatness we are reminded of our own weakness and sin). Declaration of God's offer of Forgiveness. Petition (We seek the strength God gives to lead better lives).
HYMN	Thanksgiving for God's transforming love.
LESSON	Old Testament (We now hear God's word as revealed through the Bible. Each lesson should be introduced by a few words of clarification. Could be read by a member).

(ANTHEM—when required)

LESSON	New Testament.
THE CREED	The congregation STAND to affirm their faith through a suitable Creed.
HYMN	Seeking responsive minds to hear God's Word in the sermon.
SERMON	Interpreting God's Word for our present situation.
HYMN	Applying the message of the sermon.
OFFERING	(Received by the Steward)
DOXOLOGY	The congregation STAND to sing praise to God for His many gifts in life, as the stewards bring the offering to the front.
DEDICATION	Having heard God's Word read and interpreted, we respond by dedicating our gifts, which at the same time is a symbol of the rededication of our own lives to serve Him.

CHURCH NOTICES	Going out with God's Word into the Church (These should be brief, and where possible remind us of any special need in the community).
INTERCESSIONS	Going out with God's Word into the world (We share in some of the world's needs by bringing them before God in prayer).
LORD'S PRAYER	As a summary of all our prayers, we unite to sing the prayer Jesus taught His disciples.
HYMN	Confidence and Praise.
BLESSING	Assuring us of God's presence with us as we seek to serve Him in His world.

Comment

One of us sees this as a good outline, but questions why the sermon should not sometimes be the climax of evening worship, coming in its customary Methodist place at the end. The ideal pattern for a Sunday would be to have for the principal service of the day (probably in the morning) a eucharistic structure—Ministry of the Word and Oblation—even if there were no communion. Then the second service can be an experiment, sometimes with the sermon as the *main* item, just as Wesley envisaged when he compared the Methodist preaching services to University sermons! The sermon need not always be the prophetic proclamation of one man, but may be drama, dialogue, discussion, etc.

(This comment seems to apply to the whole pattern of Sunday worship, rather than the form outlined for the service above. This form is ideal for the existing situation in many churches today. Ed.)

D. BASIC ORDER FOR CHRISTIAN WORSHIP

Source: Rev. Geoffrey Wainwright

Hymn (which may be processional)
The Approach—in the form of a dialogue between minister and people; the words will be set out in full, and will be based on Biblical material; it will usually embrace adoration, confession, forgiveness and Lord's Prayer.
Old Testament Lesson
Hymn (or Psalms, said responsively)

46

New Testament Lesson (a)

Hymn

Sermon

Hymn

Intercessions—usually grouped under Church
World
the Suffering

each service would have a full form of intercessions set out,
with provision for congregational participation (e.g. litan-
esque forms); as an alternative would be given suggested
topics for extempore prayer by the preacher, with proposals
as to how these might be punctuated by congregational parts;
the themes would bear some relation to the main theme of the
service.

Notices

Offertory

Great Prayer of Thanksgiving—
covering:

(again there would be provided both a full form and also suggestions for extempore; and the themes would be coloured by the main theme of the service)	Mighty Acts of God in creation and redemption; Activity of God in Church of past (Saints) and present; Particular blessings given in local situation. Grand Doxology (of different forms, e.g. singing 931, v8)

Hymn (which may be recessional)
Conclusion (Blessing/Dismissal for mission and service).

Comments

1. If a Psalm is to be said could it be antiphonally (i.e. alternate
half-verse) rather than responsively (i.e. alternate verses)?

2. The outstanding feature of this order is the note of thanksgiving at the end. Mr. Wainwright described the theology of this (in
'New Directions' Summer 1965):'Worship . . . is where the mighty
acts of God witnessed in scripture (and chiefly His act in Christ) are
proclaimed and where you acknowledge them with thanksgiving.'
This basic order seeks to show how this can be expressed in regular
Christian worship.

Further Comment

It would be difficult to improve upon this excellent order.

E. A SUNDAY EVENING SERVICE

Source: Stowlawn Methodist Church, USA

In this order the participation of the congregation is sought not just in words. At the beginning of the service two people light candles on the Lord's Table 'to express in symbolic fashion the presence of God in worship and a re-enactment of Our Lord's words that he is 'the light of the world'. The Bible was carried from the Table to be read at the lectern where it remained open throughout the service of the 'Word': then it was replaced on the Table. Prayers of intercession were invited from the congregation.

Introduction (by the Commentator)

We begin our worship with what Christ says to us:

> 'Anyone who wishes to be a follower of mine, must leave self behind; he must take up his cross, and come with me.'

Please stand as two members of the congregation move to the Lord's Table.

We sing the 'Hallelujahs' of Hymn No 4 at the back of the Hymn Book.

Prayer (all sitting): The response is 'Thine is the kingdom, the power, and the glory, for ever and ever'.

Hymn

Prayers (said by all)

> Most Holy and Merciful Father, we have done many wrongs and have made many mistakes. We have followed too much our own wishes. Our hearts are not right. We have paid too little attention to the call of our consciences which try to put us right. We have disobeyed your Holy Commandments. We have not done those things we ought to have done. And when we compare ourselves with your Son, Jesus Christ, there is no good in us. But Lord, have mercy upon us, poor sinners. Spare us as we confess our wrongdoing. Bring us back into your family, as we say we will strive to do better. And give us strength of mind, body, and purpose to do that which is right. Give us this pardon through Jesus Christ, Our Lord, who was born and died for our sins. We ask this with bowed heads and in His Holy Name.

M: Lord have mercy upon us.
P: Christ have mercy upon us.
M: Lord have mercy upon us.

Sentences said by the Minister, proclaiming the fact of God's forgiveness.

Psalm No 23. The response is: 'My Shepherd is the Lord—nothing indeed shall I want' (Gelineau)

Prayers of Thanksgiving (said by the Minister)

The Lord's Prayer

Scripture Reading: John 1: 1-14.

Hymn

Sermon

Hymn

Notices

Prayers for other people

Offering

Hymn (During this Hymn the 'Peace' will be given—where the Minister offers the right hand of fellowship to the congregation, in turn)

Benediction.

Please remain standing as the candles on the Lord's Table are extinguished by two members of the congregation.

Comments

1. It is good to see movement and symbolic actions. But, again, it needs to be emphasized that these must be understood by the people, otherwise it degenerates into ecclesiasticism. Perhaps the commentator's introduction could include 'Jesus said "I am the Light of the World" '. The symbolism might be improved if the two lighted candles were carried out of the church door at the end to show that God's word and light lead us out into the world's life.

2. The hymn book referred to is an American edition and some equivalent for the Hallelujahs would have to be found. It is good to see Psalms being sung in the Gelineau fashion. This involves the singing of the verses by a single singer or a choir, with the congregation singing a simple lyrical refrain. These settings of the Psalms are available from The Grail (England, 58 Sloane Street, London, SW1).

3. The service opens with a rather hard saying of Jesus. We ought not to be afraid of these but some will wonder if the very opening of the service is the place for them.

49

4. Some will be irritated by the echoes of Cranmer's General Confession in the prayer of confession. It might sound as though the General Confession was being said from a rather defective memory. Ought we to beg for mercy and ask God to spare us? Yes and No. But this prayer hardly gives time for the congregation to work that one out.

5. The prayer of thanksgiving might usefully be placed at the end as in Wainwright's order.

6. 'The Peace will be given' indicates that this is a regular practice (the advisability of which we have questioned in commenting on the Communion orders). If this is so the action will be understood by regular worshippers. The note about it on the order sheet might be amplified for the benefit of occasional members of the congregation.

Further Comment

A Psalm is an inadequate substitution for an Old Testament lesson.

3. Family Worship

THIS CHAPTER will not argue the merits of family worship. They are by now well known. So are the difficulties.

The world of the seven-year-old is peopled by hobgoblins and foul fiends; that of the teenager of seventeen by cars and girls; that of their parents by family problems and the industrial rat race. Much that happens in worship seems to have little to do with these and all the other interests that make up the congregation's daily life. Moreover, many of Methodism's traditional orders of worship—and the additions and emendations found when children are present—have no logical pattern. Too often the theology presented is naturalistic rather than incarnational.

Participation is made dependent on intellectual concentration from start to finish—difficult for adults and impossible for children. While children need an atmosphere familiar and secure in order to concentrate most easily and to know what is going to happen next, much Free Church worship gives them an impression of improvisation. The consequence is that children often equate Church-going with boredom, or else their parents are presented with little more than a children's service.

The following forms of worship have been chosen in an attempt to satisfy this wide age- and interest-range and to include symbolism, dialogue, colour, and movement; to involve the whole congregation in participation in the worship; to present a Christocentric gospel, alive and interesting, using this generation's language and thought forms; to demolish the barriers between daily life and worship; to enable children to share fully without selfconsciousness, and adults without condescension.

A. FAMILY WORSHIP AT WALKLEY

Source: Rev. David Gooderham
The crucial fact that children are happiest with the familiar has led to the choice of written orders for at least part of the worship. Here is an act of worship for the first twenty minutes of a Family Service:

1. THE PREPARATION
Leader: Good morning, everyone.
Everyone: Good morning.

Leader:	We come together today to worship God, to hear what He has to say to us, and to offer Him all that we have and are: so let us be quiet, and remember that we are in His presence as we say together
Everyone:	God be in my head and in my understanding, God be in my eyes and in my looking, God be in my mouth and in my speaking, God be in my heart and in my thinking, God be at my end and at my departing.
Leader:	Now let us praise God. (Hymn of praise, during which a group of children goes with the leader to stand round the font.)
Leader:	Where does the Christian life begin?
Children:	It begins at our baptism when God calls us His children and gives us our place in the Christian family.
Leader:	But we often fail Him; how can we be His children?
Children:	God is a loving and patient Father; if we admit our faults He will forgive us and wash away our sin.
Leader:	Then let us think for a moment about the things we have done wrong in the past week and ask His forgiveness: Pause
Everyone:	God, our Father, we have often let You down; we admit wrong thoughts, wrong words, and wrong actions; forgive these faults, make us better Christians, and help us always to be kind, reliable and cheerful, through Jesus Christ our Lord, Amen.
Leader:	Jesus says: Go in peace, your sins are forgiven. (When necessary, baptisms are administered at this point. The leader and the children return to their places).

2. THE WORD OF GOD

Leader:	Today we are going to hear about ... (the set Junior lesson) With the Bible you will see carried in ... (the visual aid) Whatever explanation is necessary is given here But first we shall sing (hymn revelant to the lesson) (As the hymn concludes, the Bible, followed by the visual aid, is carried up to the lectern.)

Reader:	Reads the lesson and concludes with:
	That is God's message for us this week.
Everyone:	Help us to understand Your message,
	help us to remember it,
	help us to live by it now and always.

Leader:	We have heard what God has to say to us;
	so let us put our trust in Him, as we stand and say
	together:
Everyone:	We believe in God, our Father,
	Who has made all things and cares for all His children;
	We believe in Jesus Christ,
	God's Son and our Master,
	Who was born in Bethelehem, baptized in the Jordan,
	and preached the coming of God's Kingdom;
	He called men to turn from self to God,
	He helped and healed all who came to Him,
	He died on a cross bearing the sin of the world,
	He rose from the grave, and is alive for ever.
	We believe in the Holy Spirit
	Who is everywhere at work,
	Who calls men and women into Christ's Church,
	and Who helps us to grow up to be citizens of God's
	Kingdom.

3. OUR RESPONSE

Leader: Now that we have put our trust in God, let us offer Him our whole lives to be used in His service, and give our money as a token of ourselves.

(The Offertory is received whilst a hymn of dedication is sung. The collectors remain standing at the table whilst the leader asks the congregation whom they wish to pray for. The requests are summed up in a brief extempore prayer, sometimes including a versicle and response.)

Everyone: The Lord's Prayer and the Grace.

The children and adults now separate for teaching, discussion, and other graded activities.

Note

Each week a visual aid appropriate to the lesson is used, e.g. real loaves and fishes. While the adults have a simple duplicated order of service, the children have their own distinctive 'worship books' made by themselves. This order is used every week, but occasionally a part of it is changed to prevent it becoming hackneyed.

Comments

1. Although this is an experimental form, the elements of worship are found in logical sequence—adoration, confession and assurance of forgiveness, the reading of the Word, the affirmation of faith, an act of dedication, the response of intercession.

2. The order combines liturgical and extempore prayer, the familiar and the new, a set pattern with opportunity for adaptation. Children are regularly reminded of the meaning of Holy Baptism, a sacrament in which they often take part. The integration of the children's instruction (in their own departments later) with the themes of the act of worship is most commendable.

3. Various details of the creed could be questioned but, taken as a whole, it seems most suitable for this congregation. (But it is not true, of course, that 'He helped and healed all who came to Him'.)

4. Would it not become almost impossible to find a weekly visual aid without descending to the gimmick? The entry of the Bible so late in the service could be overcome by bringing it through the congregation at the start of worship and then carrying it, with the visual aid, to another prominent position at the appropriate time.

5. The regular request for prayers could be used in many churches with a little persistent encouragement.

6. While the standard of language is high (modern and appropriate) it fails occasionally (e.g. 'let You down'). Some vehemently defend the 'Good mornings' but this action can be criticized for giving increased emphasis to the place of the worship-leader and ignoring the fact that the people should have been quietly worshipping while waiting for public worship to begin.

Further Comments

1. The shape of the service is excellent, but the liturgical purist may complain that Baptism should come in response to the Word and not so near to the beginning. That there are practical difficulties involved should not invariably overrule a more correct order.

2. 'All the elements of worship are found in logical sequence' (to quote a comment above), except of course the sermon or instruction, which occurs after the congregation has separated. As this instruction goes with the element of the Word it should occur in the middle, i.e. the whole congregation should re-assemble at the end. This was commended on the comment on 2.A earlier in this book. Difficulties of timing may make it impracticable, in which case the children should have their own 'part 3'. The present order gets through too much in the first twenty minutes and, apart from its effect upon the children, might deprive the sermon of its proper place in the course of worship.

3. A thanksgiving for creation and redemption is lacking.

4. The integration of the children's instruction with the themes of the act of worship is most desirable, but depends ultimately upon agreement between the lessons course for Junior Church and the official lectionary. Attempts are being made to secure this, but in the present ecumenical situation it is not altogether easy. (Nevertheless, it is possible to proceed with the Walkley scheme whether or not this top-level agreement is secured. Ed.)

5. In the attempt to be natural, the language is sometimes artificial. 'Good morning' smacks too much of the classroom and too little of divine worship. It is as likely to be caricatured as the most pious bit of Canaanite! More options should be provided to prevent this language becoming intolerable.

6. *A major comment upon the whole pattern of 'Family Church'.*

Is any pattern really satisfactory if the children leave before the sermon? It deprives the teachers of the opportunity of hearing the sermon. It is no answer to say that they can hear the evening one when the evening service is in its present state of flux. There is therefore merit in the 'American solution' in which there is a morning service slightly shorter than ours at present, with a fifteen or twenty-minute sermon. All the children except the very youngest are present, the toddlers and babies being looked after elsewhere. After an interval in which refreshments can be served (agape) there follow the periods of instruction which include adult classes, fellowship groups, and so on. As these need not include opening devotions they can be shorter than our present Sunday School sessions. The two sessions could alternately be the other way round. Such a morning is no more strenuous for children than a normal day school morning.

B. THE FIRST PART OF FAMILY WORSHIP

Source: Rev. Frank Godfrey

JESUS OUR FRIEND

All Standing

L: Jesus said 'You are my friends if you do the things I command you'

All: This is His commandment, that we love one another as He loved us. There is no greater love than this—that a man lay down his life for his friends.

Hymn

All Sit

L: We remember how Jesus made friends with children, and enjoyed being with them and talking to them.

All: All praise and thanks to God.

L: He healed the sick, comforted the sad, and cared about all the people He met.

All: All praise and thanks to God.

L: He made friends with those who were lonely, and gave courage to those who were afraid.

All: All praise and thanks to God.

L: He made friends with those who had done wrong, and was able to help them.

All: All praise and thanks to God.

L: Even when in great pain, and in the shadow of death on the cross, He was a friend to the man crucified with him.

All: All praise and thanks to God, for Jesus, a constant and wonderful friend.

L: Now let us think about our other friends.

All: We thank you, Lord, for friends who make us happy, who share our love and fun, who encourage and help us. Teach us to become good friends.

L: Who else should we make friends with?

All: Because we are friends with Jesus we shall be friends to the lonely, and the unhappy, to those who are not as strong as we are, even to those who are unfriendly to us. O Lord, help us to do this.

L: Now let us say the prayer Jesus taught his friends to say— The Lord's Prayer.

Hymn

Comments

This order has the great advantage of being Christocentric. A short prayer of confession could be naturally and appropriately introduced. The concrete ideas—rather than abstractions—will help the children, but the overall impression tends too much towards the childish for a mixed congregation.

C. TWO FORMS OF CONFESSION

One of the major difficulties of family worship—with its wide age and interest range—is the place and wording of confession and forgiveness. This problem is mirrored in the next two sections.

1. *Confession and forgiveness within family worship*
Let us pray:

> O God our Father who has bidden us to live in fellowship with one another, keep us from everything which would make us difficult to live with today.
>> Silence
>
> Help us never thoughtlessly or deliberately to speak in such a way that we hurt another's feelings or wound another's heart.
>> Silence
>
> Keep us from all impatience, all irritability and from a temper that is too quick.
>> Silence
>
> Keep us from eyes that are focused to find fault, and from a tongue which is tuned to criticize.
>> Silence
>
> Keep us from being touchy and quick to take offence and slow to forget it.
>> Silence
>
> Help us not to be stubborn and obstinate, and keep us from the selfishness which can see nothing but its own point of view and which wants nothing but its own way.
>> Silence

ALL: Accept our prayers, O Lord, and grant to us all through this day, something of the grace and beauty which shone from our Saviour Jesus Christ. Amen.

2. *Confession and forgiveness within family worship*

> Let us quietly remember Jesus and the kind of person He is. ... O God our Father, we confess that we are not like Him. He was kind and understanding. He was unselfish, daring, and brave. Only too often we quarrel. We are afraid to do what we know is right. We are too selfish to help others. We forget all about you. We admit this is the kind of people we have been this week. But we remember what Jesus told us—that if we want to be different and start again, we can. All your strength will be given us. We *would* be different people—from the bottom of our hearts. We believe that from this moment onwards you will be helping us to be more like Jesus.

ALL: Amen.

Comments

1. While the language of the first form tends to be abstract rather than concrete, it uses today's vocabulary and could be joined in intelligently by the majority of the congregation. Six periods of silence, even if short, would stretch children's concentration—but guided silent prayer of this kind could be profitably used far more widely than at present. The assurance of forgiveness should not be omitted.

2. Forgiveness is not explicitly pronounced in the second form, either, but it is accepted by the congregation on their affirmation of faith. This is one aspect of the commendably positive approach of this form. The weakness is that for a mixed congregation it veers too much towards the childish.

Further Comments

The assurance of forgiveness is by no means explicit enough in the first form. The second form has some verbal infelicities.

D. AN OUTLINE NOT NEEDING AN ORDER SHEET

Source: Rev. Wallace White

Most of these acts of worship have necessitated a written sheet for congregational use. Here is a suggested order for churches which will not or cannot use a written service, yet want a liturgically good order as a basis for new ideas.

1	Prayer of confession and assurance of forgiveness	Confession here because (a) not too much emphasis on sin when children of all ages present (b) we should 'leave our sins at the church door'. Sin dealt with, we can then go on to:
2	Hymn of adoration and worship	
3	Responsive prayers of thanksgiving	
4	Instruction for younger children	Without this they receive no direct teaching
5	Hymn	
6	Lesson (OT)	
7	Lesson (NT)	Read by a member of a church family
8	Hymn	

9	Sermon	About 10 minutes if the service is not to last longer than 50-60 minutes
10	Notices	The response of the family of the Church to the message of God
11	Offertory	Collected by members of a family
12	Dedication of offertory, and intercessions (responsive)	Subjects of prayer sent in by families or children before the service or collected at the door on arrival
13	Hymn of praise and thanksgiving	Not dedication—my giving of *myself* to God—but ending with *God* and *His* glory
14	Blessing	'Go forth into the world . . .'

Practical Notes: (Numbers refer to numbers in the outline service)

1. The basic difficulty is to find a form of words that is not too childish for adults or meaningless to children and yet gives each the assurance of forgiveness.

2. To prevent the congregation spending their prayer-time waiting for their cue, a fairly long versicle is useful. But the response must be short and easily memorable. Even then a strong lead must be given, the leader saying (at least at first) the congregational response also. Regular use of responsive prayers, or the use of the same response, soon overcomes the difficulties. Too many items should be avoided, especially with children present. Five is perhaps the maximum. There are a number of ways of leading responsive prayer. For a congregation not used to this method, the following is helpful:

Leader: For all these gifts, let us bless the Lord
People: Father accept our praise

or

Leader: We bless You, O Father
People: With all our heart and mind

or

Leader: For . . . let us praise the Lord
People: We thank you, O God

3. Beware of verbosity and irrelevance! Five minutes is ample. The sermon subject can be explained at the children's level; or the meaning of the lessons and their context. The period of the Church Year may choose the subject. The significance of an aspect of the church or its architecture (e.g. the pulpit, Communion Table, font) can be used. Generalized moral exhortation is anathema!

4. Children need an opportunity to make a response. A hymn or prayer can provide this.

5/6. Participation by the congregation can be increased by antiphonal reading of a Psalm or a passage from the back of the hymn book. Otherwise, modern translations essential. Both lessons can be read by members of the same family.

The rest of the service is response to the message of God read and expounded earlier: notices—response of giving time; offertory—response of giving possessions; intercessions—response of love, etc.; hymn—response of praise, faith, thanksgiving; blessing—response of return as God's people to God's world.

12. If the leader knows the children well, they may suggest subjects for intercession there and then; better still, the congregation can be trained to do so.

14. Dismissal to live as Christ's people in Christ's strength in Christ's world (from the 1928 Prayer Book).

Other Variations

The above order is only an outline. Many variations can be used.

(a) In the prayers, God can be addressed as 'You'.

(b) For 'sermon' read 'drama, play-reading, dialogue, tape, filmstrip' according to taste, conviction, or courage!

(c) When younger children are not present, the children's instruction can be omitted and the sermon divided into two parts—a great help to many teenage listeners.

(d) The Bible can be carried through the congregation to the pulpit/lectern at the opening of the service. The Bible can be carried into the centre of the congregation for the reading of the Word of God.

(e) Modern hymns and/or modern tunes can be used. Modern words can be sung to the tunes of well-known secular songs without congregational practice, e.g. Ylvisaker's version of John 1: 1-8 sung to 'Michael row the boat ashore'.

Comments

The merit of this service is that it uses a liturgically accurate form as a vehicle for experiment. It would need the addition of varied material to make it alive, but notes are added as suggestions making for elasticity whilst retaining the logical form. Some would object to starting with confession, but there are many precedents, so this is an arguable point.

Further Comments

If this kind of service is to be held once a month or once a quarter, the extreme brevity of the sermon may be tolerated. But this is a very valuable outline offering sound and positive guidance.

E. FAMILY SERVICE NEEDING AN ORDER SHEET

Source: Rev. Wallace White

Minister:	We will stand as the Word of God is brought among us (A family brings the Bible from the back of the church, through the congregation to the pulpit/lectern.)
Prayer:	O God, our Father, you are with us in our daily lives in the world. But we meet together now to praise you and to be instructed and strengthened by you. Speak to each one of us and empower us with the Holy Spirit that we may follow more accurately and enthusiastically in the days ahead.
Hymn of praise:	e.g. 93, 83, 588
Scripture reading:	The Bible is carried by one member of a family, accompanied by the rest of the family, into the congregation. Matthew 25: 31-45 (Modern translation)
Film or filmstrip:	Illustrating today's world of split families: (Vietnam; National Children's Home; refugees; broken homes)
Prayer of confession: (Minister)	This is your world, Lord. But this is what we have made of it. We are utterly ashamed of ourselves. Yet we who are before you in this service feel too helpless and unimportant to make any difference. We cannot alter the policies of the nations; and we are not people of great gifts or influence. We see the need of the world's families—and we feel frustrated. Yet we remember that it is not the people who sing your praises but the people who do your will who are your real followers. So we are praying now, in this service, that you will show us what we can do for these families whom you love so dearly.
Hymn for guidance:	e.g. 298 v. 1-4; 301; 895; 289

Explanation (Minister or layman)	of local needs of local efforts to help e.g. Christian Aid; Voluntary Service Overseas; OXFAM, etc. Appeal for ideas: 'In the pews are sheets of paper. In the next prayer for guidance write down what you think we as a Church can do. Then put these papers in the plate with the offertory and they will be passed on to our leaders for action. You can make, too, some decision about what you yourself can do.'
Prayer for guidance: (Minister)	O Lord Jesus Christ, you lived in a family. You know the needs of family life. And you know, too, what the world's families lack. In the quietness, let us know what you would have us do for them.
Hymn of faith:	e.g. 249, 272
Notices:	(the incongruity of some may put a question mark against them)
Offertory:	Collected by a church family; dedication followed by:
Intercessions:	(After each of the following biddings, there can follow a short written or extempore prayer by the Minister, completed by this versicle and response, or some other.) Let us pray for the families of the world. . . . Let us pray for the family of the world Church. . . . Let us pray for the families of our town. . . . A prayer of quiet in which we will pray silently for any whose special needs we know. . . .
Minister: People:	O Father, answer this prayer According to your loving wisdom
Hymn of dedication	to the service of God and men: e.g. 795, 810, 578, 400
Blessing:	Go forth into the world. . . . (1928 Prayer Book).

Comments

The sermon, apparently omitted, is in fact contained in two parts, filmstrip and explanation. This is an example of how, behind the unfamiliar actions of this service, there is a good liturgical order. The church leaders would have to know what was planned beforehand and agree to consider suggestions sent to them.

Children would find some of the language difficult, and very little children might find the whole act of worship too horrific.

Only a small church or hall could use normal film strip apparatus. As visual aid material goes out of date so quickly, no suggestions are made.

Summary

The aim of this chapter was partly frustrated by the material received. Much of it contained helpful ideas, but lacked any basic liturgical order. Some kept a logical order but showed no awareness of modern insights into children and their worship. But the large quantity of material received, both from laymen and ministers, is proof that helpful experimentation is not for the liturgical expert only. Given basic knowledge of the right ordering of worship, many more people could and should produce interesting and satisfying orders of worship in which all the family could take part.

4. The Christian Festivals

A PERSONAL PLEA *Brian Frost*

THE SCRIPTS submitted in this section were disappointing—none were submitted for Easter or Pentecost. One or two were submitted for Ascension time and one for the Feast of Christ the King, interpreting Ascension in terms of Christ's Lordship over creation.

They raised the crucial problem for modern worship: how, especially in the Christian Festivals, can you write material in which the congregation can take part whilst avoiding an out-dated and unmeaningful language pattern? Take for example an incarnational sequence 'God in a garage', sent in by an enterprising Youth Club in which Mary and Joseph left for Egypt on a scooter. The story was told in a number of scenes, interspersed with modern carols written specially by a member of the local club. The wise men become scientists in their observatory:

> To the feet of Jesus,
> Science would we bring,
> Satellites and test tubes,
> Oh, atomic King.
> Help us use these forces,
> Peace on earth to gain,
> Food for hungry people,
> Healing for our pain.

So far a genuine attempt has been made to interpret the narrative. But the outcome—God coming from outer space—put the story finally back in fairy-tale dressing which lent an air of unreality to all that had gone before.

Is there any way out of this? Perhaps I can describe in some detail an Easter script I was involved in producing in my local church two years ago. The script centred on three people—one a humanist, one a Christian who was fairly articulate, the third a rather hazy woman who felt she ought to attend church. The three of them argued about a dramatic presentation which went on before them and the congregation. The argument was about the meaning of love. It centred on the life of Marilyn Monroe, who took her life because she had been deprived of love in childhood and adult life, and Christ, whose life was taken from him because his power of loving threatened the established forces of the time.

First there was her mother walking down the aisles, talking about how Marilyn came to be born (establishing that she was conceived without love). It became clear that though she craved for love she was continually deprived of it, because she could not relate herself to others. Worse, the world of the cinema, big business and even her husbands, exploited her. In the end she took her life, or was, if you like, crucified by herself and by society.

Secondly there was Mary, Christ's mother, explaining how it was that Jesus came to die. He had related himself so positively to what was good and right in human life that he upset the religious leaders, the political leaders, and even his followers. His death had a kind of inevitability about it, just as Marilyn Monroe's had. The difference was that his kind of loving (at the other end of the human scale) produced death because of a threat to the egos of others.

The interplay between these two ideas was commented on by the three viewers, who exchanged ideas of death and life and love with each other. Did Christ have a power of love which even death could not quench? How could this be stated without the conventional trimmings of the Easter story? This was the crucial problem. In the end recourse was had to Dylan Thomas's poem 'And Death Shall Have No Dominion' which asserts that in the end even death is overcome.

Slowly the truth of the central Christian affirmation dawned on the three arguers and the climax of the worship came when the humanist left the pulpit in incredulity—that the Christians affirm love, despite all the evidence in the world to disprove it. The Christian rather haltingly went to the pulpit.

But how could the congregation enter into this dialogue with the three, apart from their identification with the argument? This was where folk songs were used. The death of Marilyn Monroe was poetically put across by a folk singer who sang 'Who Killed Norma Jean?'—the gist of the song being that it was all of us. This linked with the idea that we all in some way had a stake in the killing of Jesus. Other songs were included which the congregation were asked to join in, using the words provided on a printed sheet.

The most moving moment of the whole service was a beat group playing 'Stranger on the Shore' (the Acker Bilk number) very quietly, while a member of the Youth Club read straightforwardly the Resurrection narrative of Jesus and the disciples on the shore after Easter. Yet even here was one cheating? Was one falling back on a supernaturalist description even though the resurrection idea had been set in the universality of love which overcomes all?

To say that the service was a success would be making a judgment in a wrong idiom. Certainly there were objections—particularly about Marilyn Monroe's centrality. Our reluctance to face the real world in worship became evident. What was clear was that one or two people came to worship for the first time in their lives, so that the discussion afterwards was one of the most lively I have ever experienced in a church hall. It had an air of reality about it because there was a searching, a conflict in people's minds about their worship. A new approach to worship (through dialogue and deliberate questioning) had taken the place of the traditional statement of an accredited fact by the authoritarian Father figure in the pulpit.

The sequel was sadder. There was a demand from the Leader's Meeting that no more experiments be tried on Christian Festivals, thereby showing the disastrous divorce between worship and reality that pervades much or most of church life, relegating such services to the periphery of worship instead of putting them at the centre. I remain convinced, however, that worship will never again become real for people unless there is tension and dialogue and doubt included in it, a wrestling with faith. That wrestling with faith and doubt must surely be more than evident at the heart of the Christian affirmations—the Festivals.

I would accordingly like to see Palm Sunday linked with the entry of modern politicians into their city as Jesus entered the city of Jerusalem. One can imagine one of Kennedy's motor-cades going round Chicago or New York on an electioneering trip; one can see De Gaulle's wooing of the Latin American cities on his triumphal tour there. One could link this with May Day in Peking where the crowds throng the streets to trumpet-in the now-fading revolution. Here, surely, is fruit for a writer to use this part of the Christian narrative so that it makes sense.

Another writer might like to work out a modern Pentecost, using the Biblical material about language, a new community of the Spirit, which is the universal and catholic church. He would perhaps see the struggle of the United Nations through its rival power groups as the possible agent through which the Holy Spirit now works to bring all men into unity. He might be able to hint that through science and technology modern man is being united far more quickly than he can understand. If he is perceptive perhaps he can then link the whole growth of the ecumenical movement to Pentecost, as the Churches together grope after that experience which alone can unite the broken nations, overcome the barriers of language, and bring men into a joyous affirmation of the unity of all men in the love and truth of Christ.

It was, I think, George Macleod who said that August 6th—the traditional date of the Transfiguration Festival—was also the date of the dropping of the atomic bomb on Japan. Perhaps if in previous years this aspect of the life of Christ had been more related to a

Christian doctrine of aggression, such influence as the Churches have across the world could have altered the course of the affairs of men more positively?

There is no reason why the Festivals themselves should not become the focus for realistic worship, where we meet the world at greater depth, not escaping from it or aiming to go from it to 'take God to' a world where he is already. All that is needed is the courage and determination to carry through this revolution in a thorough and creative way, because we are reflecting a new way of being a Christian, with a spirituality stemming from the world, not taken to it—in other words, because we have pondered deeply the meaning of being in the world on behalf of God, and being before God on behalf of the world.

A Further Comment

Liturgy is often at its most conservative on the great days of the Christian year, but it is these days also which have been enriched with supplementary services such as the blessing of the Crib or the Palm Sunday procession, which precede or follow, but do not replace, the customary service. I feel that the people have a right to the familiar services at these times, and am glad that several of these in this section are obviously devised as supplementary devotions. This does not apply so much to Maundy Thursday, for Methodism has never really settled for any particular form of service on that day and a complete new service may well be used then.

A.   ADVENT SUNDAY MORNING

Source: Rev. Norwyn Denny
This morning service is for use on the Sundays of Advent. When the first Sunday in Advent falls in December the Service is Holy Communion and the alternative ending is followed.
Opening Prayers . . . Sentences
   Guided prayers of Confession and Thanksgiving

Hymn 242: 'Come, thou long-expected Jesus'
  The Lighting of the Advent Candle. (One if First Advent, two
     if Second Advent and so on.)
     (If a family can be responsible each week it helps the
     idea of family worship, for families are encouraged to
     do the same at home each Sunday in Advent.)

A parent says: 'One candle to remind us of the prophets, who believed in God during dark days, and looked forward to the coming of Christ.'
(On other weeks: 'The second for John the Baptist, who called men to change their way of living to prepare for the coming of Christ.' 'The third for Mary, who simply and gladly responded to the call of God.' 'The fourth for us as we join with them in looking for the coming of Christ.')

Someone reads: 'The people who walked in darkness have seen a great light. Those who dwelt in a land of deep darkness, on them has light shined.'
(On other weeks: 'The light shines in the darkness and the darkness has not overcome it. There was a man sent from God whose name was John. He came to bear witness to the light that all might believe through him.' 'And Mary said, "Behold the handmaid of the Lord; be it unto me according to thy word." ' 'With all these witnesses to faith around us . . . we must throw off every hindrance, every sin to which we cling, and run with resolution the race on which we are entered, our eyes fixed on Jesus.')

Then this prayer is said: 'O God our Father, we thank you for the faithful men of every age. We pray that we too may have faith in spite of the darkness of our times, and may look for the coming of Christ into the world of our day. Amen.'
(On other weeks: 'O God our Father, we thank you for the witness of John the Baptist. Help us so to expect the coming of our Lord, that we may ever be true members of his Church.' 'O God our Father, we thank you for the joyful obedience of Mary. Help us to honour her lowly grace and to share in the humility which does not despise the Christ who comes as a child, born in a stable.' 'O God our Father, we thank you for our place among all who would worship Christ the King. Help us now at Christmas to do as he commands, to care for our neighbours as we do for ourselves.')

The Collect for the day
(During the lighting of the candle(s) the parent says 'one candle . . .' etc.)

Old Testament Lesson or Epistle

The Te Deum

New Testament Lesson or Gospel

The Benedictus (Even where Morning Prayer is not being used, it is valuable to use the Benedictus during Advent.)

The Sermon

The Creed

Hymn 257: 'O come, O come, Immanuel'

> (in the service of Morning Prayer)
>> Versicles and responses . . .
>> The Three collects
>> The other prayers
>> Concerns of the Church (notices)
>> Prayers of Concern
>> The Offertory

> (in the service of Holy Communion)
>> Concerns of the Church
>> The Offertory (bread, wine, and money)
>> Prayers for the Church and the World
>> (Dearly beloved in the Lord)
>> Comfortable Words
>> Sursum Corda . . .
>> Prayer of Humble Access—'We do not presume . . .'
>> Rest of Communion

Hymn 264: 'Lo! he comes with clouds descending'
> Benediction

Comments

A simple service involving church families from Notting Hill which emphasizes movement and colour. It also links movement with symbol, with some brief Biblical insight. Some will doubt whether the retention of the form of a kind of Morning Prayer really enables people to worship from within their present language and patterns. Others will find the evident structure and rhythm liturgically helpful for worship, reminding them of the continuous tradition of the Church and bringing a wholeness they had perhaps not felt before.

Further Comments

1. It is good to find concern for the world, and the family life of our time, linked with the great Christian tradition.

2. The idea of putting this candle ceremony at the beginning of Morning Prayer or Holy Communion is sound—presumably the two services would not be set out on the same paper. The Psalms are omitted from Morning Prayer, which is regrettable because this service is so bound up with the corporate recitation of the Psalter.

3. Is the service actually linked closely enough with the full meaning of Advent? Where is the eschatology and the news of the final hope in Christ? It is true that Hymn 264 comes in, but almost as an after-thought.

4. 'Darkness of our time' is now a cliché, and is certainly not accepted by very many people.

B. ADVENT

Source: Rev. Donald May

Introit: Hymn 83: 'Of the Father's love begotten', vv. 1, 3, 4.

Explanatory introduction and any necessary announcements
Collect and Lord's Prayer

Hymn 257:   'O come, O come Immanuel'

Part I *He that has come*

Reader: Let us hear of him that should come, as he was foretold by the prophets. (Selections from Messianic prophecies—Isaiah 40: 1-5; Malachi 3: 1-3; Zechariach 9: 9; Isaiah 9: 2, 6, 7.)

Narrator: But what was the reality? Most people failed to notice this birth, for it seemed a happening of no significance. If they had known they would have avoided it.

Common people: We do not wish anything to happen. . . .
(Spoken by   (See note, p.73).
2 voices)

Narrator: Of those to whom the significance of the birth was revealed, some were shepherds, the outcasts of the community, despised because their work made it impossible for them to carry out their religious duties properly. The shepherds were awake, but how many others were?

Hymn:	Advent Carol (tune: Forest Green)

1 It's a weary road from Nazareth
With a baby in the womb
And Joseph fell asleep as soon
As he had found them room.
The invaded cows were restless as
They waited for the dawn,
But Joseph went on sleeping as
The Son of God was born.

2 The shepherds had their flocks to watch
And were too cold for rest.
The kings swayed in their saddles as
Their camels plodded west.
And some were called by angels,
Others the star had drawn,
But Joseph went on sleeping as
The Son of God was born.

3 We hear the story every year,
Perhaps it might sink in,
But Christmas is a family time,
And we have closed the inn.
Again the angel gospel sounds,
Again the skies are torn,
And shall we go on sleeping as
The Son of God is born?

Narrator:	The feelings of those to whom the real meaning of the birth was revealed may have been far less comfortable than we may imagine. What for example did Simeon, the priest, feel?
Simeon:	Grant us thy peace. . . . (See note, p.73)
Narrator:	Kings, wise men who were Jews, neither by birth nor by religion, learned of the birth and came to pay homage.
King:	A cold coming we had of it. . . . (See note, p.73)
Hymn 132:	'As with gladness men of old'
Narrator:	Through the kings news came to another king, Herod. His reaction to something that could upset the unstable peace between his country and Rome was a policy of ruthless extermination.

71

Speaker:	(at back of congregation) And what of ourselves? Do we acknowledge the possibility that God may be revealing himself to us through those outside his Church, whether intellectuals or workers, rulers or outcasts? Is our reaction that of Simeon, to pray that the old pattern of religious life will last out our lifetime? Or are we like Herod—violently opposed to anything that threatens our security, our comfort, or our peace of mind? Dare we accept the action of God in his world today?
	(Pause)
	Part II *He that shall come*
Hymn 264:	'Lo! he comes with clouds descending'
Narrator:	If we look back to an event in the past, do we also look forward to an equally far off day in the future, the second coming of Christ? Is this how we envisage the second coming?
Reader:	Apocalyptic readings (Malachi 4: 1; Joel 2:28-31; Revelation 20: 12; 1 Thessalonians 4: 16-17; 1 Corinthians 15: 51-52.)

The readings continue in a different taped voice against a musical background.

Narrator:	But when we consider how Christ himself taught us about his second coming, our attitude changes.
Reader:	Matthew 25: 31ff
Hymn 895: or 259:	'Where cross the crowded ways of life' 'And art thou come with us to dwell?'
	Part III *He that is coming*
Narrator:	It is one thing to think of the one who came in the past, and who shall come in the future, it is another to think of him in the present, but in fact he comes to us whenever we see these needs—the hungry, the homeless, the poor, the sick, the imprisoned. As Christmas approaches, let us remember how St. Francis invited the people of Assisi to see a crib, and then, snatching a baby from its embarrassed mother's arms, placed it in the crib and cried:

St. Francis:	Behold your God, a poor and helpless child, the ox and ass beside him. Your God is of your flesh, he dwells in you, in every man, for all men are your brothers.
Narrator:	How do we see these needs today?
2nd Reader:	(Reads extract from newspapers about world and local problems).
Offertory	
Hymn 137:	'In the bleak midwinter'.
Narrator:	How do we react? Not with gold, or lambs, nor with a vague sentimental idea of bringing our hearts, but with our whole lives, as they really are (Members of the congregation come up with symbols of their daily lives: I bring my life as housewife, student, mechanic, nurse, etc.)
Narrator:	How do we react? (Silent meditation)
Speaker:	(At back) 'Help me to say yes' (Prayer by Michel Quoist).
Narrator:	Blessing

Notes:

The carol was composed by John Lansley, a member of the Notting Hill Church. The three major speeches (Common People, Simeon, and The King) are from T. S. Eliot, *Murder in the Cathedral*, pp.18, 19; 'A song for Simeon' and 'Journey of the Magi', taken from *Collected Poems* 1909-1935 (Faber & Faber).

The final prayer is from page 93 of Michel Quoist's *Prayers of Life*. (Gill & Co.).

In this particular service the speeches were mostly made from the front of the Church, but obviously there would be much scope for drama and movement.

Comments

1. A mixture of old and new is contained in this service, lacking a little in uniform content (it uses both T. S. Eliot and folk-style). But it does try to link the past coming of Christ with his present rule by using readings from the newspaper and asking members of the congregation to offer what they actually use in their daily life. But, apart from that, does the congregation have enough to do? Perhaps different members could read the Biblical passages and the Quoist passage? They may have difficulty with the tune of the carol.

2. Part 1: Undoubtedly the best part. Why doesn't a crowd actually read the speech for 'Common People'? The final speech of the Speaker lacks punch and does not relate to what has gone before.

3. Part II: Not so convincing. Matthew 25 is surely not the sum total of Jesus' teaching about his second coming. Perhaps more reference to the consummation of all things rather than the difficult phrase 'the second coming'. It cannot be confined as here to Matthew 25—the Biblical teaching of history is wider than this.

4. Part III. Here the narrator mentions Jesus' coming through human needs, then goes to St. Francis where Jesus' coming is identified simply with human existence; then switches back to human needs again. But then when the crunch question comes 'How do we react?' we have the answer 'With our whole lives, as they really are'. A clear expression of total commitment to the person and claim of Christ is needed *before* we present our symbols. Otherwise we decry 'a vague sentimental idea of bringing our hearts' only to replace it with an equally vague sentimental idea of bringing our daily jobs. Perhaps, too, the Quoist prayer should precede a person's offering of himself.

5. Was it wise to use T. S. Eliot (with his considerable perception) in Part I, without similar perceptive material for Parts II and Part III? The sum total may be to ask too many questions and create too much intensity.

Further Comments

1. The first part concentrates too much on the Christmas story and not enough on what God did in Christ. I am sorry for poor Simeon—I always thought he said the *right* thing.

2. The second part is obviously inadequate. Liturgies of this persuasion must get down to *interpreting* this area of thought by projecting the final victory of life into the future and then at once bringing it back into the present again.

D. A DIALOGUE SERMON FOR CHRISTMAS

Narrator 1:   In the sixth month the angel Gabriel was sent from God to a town in Galilee called Nazareth, with a message for a girl betrothed to a man named Joseph, a descendant of David; the girl's name was Mary. The Angel went in and said to her, 'Greetings, most favoured one! The Lord is with you.'

(continues to read)

74

(Janet and Bernie from seats in the congregation)

Janet: They do go on, don't they?

Bernie: How many more times do you think? How many
                more years are they going to go on churning out
                this stuff?

Janet: Well it keeps them happy. They must get some
                sort of kick out of it, I suppose.

Bernie: You're joking of course. (*Shouts to Narrator II*).
                Hey mister, look at this lot. They don't want to
                know. Can't you see they're bored right up to the
                eyeballs with all these fairy stories?

Janet: (*in a whisper*) Shut up, Bernie. Let them alone.
                They're not doing you any harm. You're always
                poking your big nose into things that don't con-
                cern you.

Bernie: Yes that's right. Now beat it, Bird, and leave me
                alone.

(*Narrators here become distracted by the conversation and look at
Janet and Bernie*)

Janet: (*on the way to another seat*) Always looking for
                trouble you are

Bernie: (*to narrators*) She's such a *nice* girl—comes from a
                good home you know.

Narrator II: The Angel went in and said to her, 'Greetings,
                most favoured one! The Lord is with you.' But
                she was deeply troubled by what he said and
                wondered what this greeting might mean.

Bernie: Nothing

Narrator II: Did you say something?

Bernie: You bet I said something. Those words 'The Lord
                is with you', they mean nothing, nothing at all.
                Those words are stupid, mister, and you ought to
                be locked up for saying them.

Narrator II: Why do you say that?

Bernie: Because no one's with anybody in this life, see.
                You're on your tod, mister.
                (*Goes down aisle towards Narrator*)

Narrator II: And what does that mean?
Bernie: On your tod: on your own. That's the trouble
                with you religious people. You can't stand on

	your own two feet and go it alone. You've just got to invent some God, who comes along and rescues you from the mess you're in.
Narrator II:	You haven't got any troubles, I suppose?
Bernie:	I didn't say that did I? I don't need no one, mate, I can look after myself.
Narrator II:	You were a baby once. Remember? You needed help then.
Bernie:	But did I get it? Yes, sir, did I get it? That is the question.
Narrator I:	This is the story of a baby.
Bernie:	It's a story *for* babies.
Narrator I:	Then the angel said to her, 'Do not be afraid, Mary, for God has been gracious to you; you shall conceive and bear a son, and you shall give Him the name Jesus. He will be great; He will bear the title Son of the Most High; the Lord God will give Him the throne of his ancestor David, and He will be King over Israel for ever; His reign shall never end.'
Bernie:	He got it wrong didn't he?
Narrator I:	(*exasperated*) Who got it wrong?
Bernie:	That angel bloke.
Narrator I:	You mean the Angel Gabriel.
Bernie:	That's him.
Narrator II:	And how did he get it wrong?
Bernie:	Well, this Jesus guy didn't become so great after all, did he? He came to a very early and nasty end; yes, very nasty indeed.

The dancers come through the hall accompanied by dramatic music, and the continuing chant of 'Crucify Him! Crucify Him!' etc. A Jesus figure stumbles before them being flogged. Eventually they reach the stage and dance a crucifixion scene.

Jesus:	Father, forgive them, they do not know what they are doing.
Woman 1:	If you're the Son of God, why don't you come down and save yourself?
Man 1:	He saved others, but he can't save himself. King of Israel indeed!

76

Woman 2:	We'll believe you mate if you get down off that cross.
Man 2:	Let God come and rescue him, if he wants him.
Jesus:	My God, my God, why have you forsaken me? (*He cried out loud and dies. Silence*)
Bernie:	Poor deluded swine! (*To Narrator*) Well, there was no God with him, mister, was there? Ended up on his tod—and that's where we all end up. But he was soft, he let them get him and stick him up there on a bit of wood as helpless as a newborn baby. You've got to be hard in this life, stand up for your rights, know what you want and grab it, and if anyone stands in your way smash them down. He never grew up, he was as helpless as a little child.
Narrator II:	A little child. And so Joseph went up to Judaea from the town of Nazareth in Galilee, to be registered at the city of David, called Bethlehem, because he was of the House of David by descent; and with him went Mary who was betrothed to him. She was pregnant, and while they were there the time came for her child to be born, and she gave birth to a son, her firstborn. She wrapped him round and laid him in a manger, because there was no room for them to lodge in the house.
Bernie:	There's no room for anyone in this world. You're always being crowded out, ignored. People just don't want to know. So you've just got to force them to know, see! (smashes fist into hand).
Narrator I:	No, I don't see.
Bernie:	You take my old woman, for instance.
Narrator I:	You mean your mother?
Bernie:	My mother—yeah, that's right, my mother. Well, I was her fourth and by that time she just didn't want to know, see, she couldn't be bothered. I was a nuisance. I got to feel guilty just for being around. But at least she knows I'm around. Every so often I drop things she values—accidental like —you know, little knick-knacks. (*Aggressively to Narrator II*) Get in there and make a noise, is what I say. Bang on their doors,

smash their lamp posts, make yourself a social problem, and meet the big boys—you know, the magistrates and all the crowd.

Anyway, what about all these fairy tales, mate? You'd better get on with it.

Narrator II: An angel of the Lord appeared to Joseph in a dream, and said to him, 'Rise up, take the child and his mother and escape with them to Egypt, and stay there until I tell you; for Herod is going to search for the child to do away with him.'

Bernie: Yeah, there are plenty of people like that around. Oh, they won't stick a knife in your guts—that's against the law, that is. No they do away with you in a different way. They're not interested in you as a person. Of course you're very useful in many ways—as a cog in a machine.

(*Sid stands up in congregation*).

Sid: What's all this dribble I can hear you spouting, Bernie?

Bernie: Mind your own business, I'm having a chat with this gentleman here.

Sid: Yes, so I hear, and I wish you'd come and sit down.

Bernie: (*to Narrator II, pointing at Sid*) This is a world of faceless people, mate. You can't pin them down as being any different to anyone else. They look the same, talk the same, and behave the same. They wear the same clothes, buy the same records, go to the same clubs, and work in the same factories.

Sid: What are you on about, Bernie?

Bernie: Go away, mate.

Sid: You coming down the club? Come on, Bernie, let's go.

Bernie: You know I've been banned from that lousy joint now, don't you? They tried to get me to go to *this* kind of set up. But they don't really want to know —all they want is pew fodder—that's all. Come to Church and we'll let you shuffle to The Stones on Wednesday night. Well they can have that. All they are interested in is filling up their crummy pews on Sunday morning. The next time I come down to that place will be to smash it up.

Sid:	Well I'll see you at school tomorrow then? (*Exit*)
Bernie:	I think I'll be off sick tomorrow.
Narrator II:	Whatever are you going to be sick for?
Bernie:	Because school's another place where you don't count. All they want is nice little boys who do what teacher says, are ever so polite, and say 'Yes, sir; No sir;' at the right times. School's marvellous for sheep, but if you're an individual, don't try mate, because they don't want to know.
Narrator II:	Where *can* you feel at home? You hate everything —the whole world.
Bernie:	That's right. Still it's better to feel something, even hate. Look at that Sid bloke. He's never felt anything in his guts, in all his fifteen years. He hasn't got the energy. I ask you. What a thing to be—washed out at fifteen and ready to do a good job in the local pea factory for the rest of his life. No, I reckon I'm like that Jesus nipper—out in the flaming Egyptian desert somewhere—a sort of refugee.
Narrator II:	So you're out on a limb then?
Bernie:	Yes, that's right, on my tod—homeless and lonely—but I've still got a lot of fight left in me.
Narrator II:	You're not alone in being homeless. Listen!
Voice of Jesus:	(*Cry from the cross*) My God, My God, why have you forsaken me?
Narrator I:	Jesus gave a loud cry, and breathed his last. And when the centurion who was standing opposite him saw how he died, he said 'Truly this man was a Son of God'.
Narrator II:	That is the God who is with us. We are not alone in our homelessness. He has made our homelessness his home.
Narrator I:	And he shall be called 'Emmanuel', a name which means 'God with us'.
Narrator II:	When we realize God is with us, then we shall realize that our real home is with him. If we are crucified with Christ, by sharing his homelessness, his loneliness, his feeling of being forsaken,

79

	then we shall rise with Christ, to know the God of love who is our real home.
Narrator I:	Suddenly Jesus was there in their path. He gave them his greeting, and they came up and clasped his feet, falling prostrate before him.
Narrator II:	The time came that Herod died, and an angel of the Lord appeared in a dream to Joseph in Egypt and said to him 'Rise up, take the child and his mother, and go with them to the land of Israel, for the men who threatened the child's life are dead.' (*To Bernie*) Are you still afraid of being crowded out, of not being noticed, of being homeless?
Bernie:	Was I afraid?
Narrator II:	You said that one must force people to notice. Surely you only do that if you are frightened they won't?
Bernie:	(*ironically*) Well it doesn't really matter any more does it? This Jesus of yours had nowhere to lay his head did he? Foxes have their lairs, birds of the air have their nests, but the Son of Man has nowhere to lay his head. No I'm not on my tod anymore am I? I never realized it before but I've got a home with the homeless ones and this God of yours—he's one of us ain't he? So why should you worry and why should we worry? Yeah, that's right, why should we worry? (*Goes off thoughtfully*).

Notes:

This took place at Senacre Secondary Modern School, Maidstone, for the senior pupils and parents. It included carols which have been cut out. Because it was written for a school environment, the script has been edited.

The dance mime of the crucifixion was performed by fourth-year girls, the music taken from Moussorgsky's 'Pictures in an exhibition'. Voices from the cross and crowd were superimposed via the tape recorder.

Comments

1. The dialogue is about the representatives of the middle class (the 'religious') resisting the symbol of social maladjustment. Slowly the façade cracks, and both parties become real. But the conversion of Bernie at the end is unconvincing.

2. The dialogue introduces elements of doubt, conflict, etc., leaving many areas jagged and unsettled. This is all to the good, for it helps to heighten tension and expose us all the more effectively to the anxiety of the Christmas story, so often covered in sugar and cream and womb-attitudes.

D. *KING SUPREME*
(CHRISTMAS OR EPIPHANY)

Source: Rev. Richard Jones

A Christmas Service requiring a darkened Church. A Nativity setting is placed in the centre. During the opening readings Mary and Joseph take up their places there, then, as the Service proceeds, more and more groups assemble on either side.

Call to Worship

Opening Hymn

Prayer

Lord's Prayer

Announcements

Hymn (and Offering taken)

    (*Lights steadily dimmed as three Bible-readers speak from pulpit*)

B.1:	Genesis 1: 1*f*
B.2:	Genesis 1: 27 and 2: 15-17
B.3:	Genesis 3: 4, 6, 8
B.1:	Isaiah 59. 9, 10, 14
B.2:	Isaiah 59. 15b, 16a
B.3:	Ezekiel 37. 23b, 24a

    (*The Modern Voice speaks from the balcony*)

M.V.:   We would like a government for the whole world, one single voice whom we could trust, one who would command respect from East and West, from black and white, from rich nation and poor nation. But there is no such person, no such leader, no such king. We need a king supreme.

    (*The two commentators speak from the choir*)

C.1:   But the Jews had a king! Herod the Great. Born sixty-three years before Jesus. A tall, magnificent man. A born leader.

C.2:   He had ten wives, eight sons, six daughters.

C.1:   He was a fine ruler, firm and strong. A brilliant soldier.

C.2:   But cruel and ruthless. During his reign he murdered his uncle, his mother-in-law, his brother-in-law, his son-in-law, then his wife, then three of his own sons.

B.1:   God sends the King supreme.
(Spotlight fastens on the Nativity tableau. Mary and Joseph are admiring the baby Jesus).

B.2:   Isaiah 9: 2

B.3:   Isaiah 9: 6

Solo: Two verses of Hymn 83: 'Of the Father's love begotten'.
Exuberant dance by children before the King.
Enter angels singing Hymn 117: 'Hark! the herald-angels'.
Enter carol singers.

B.1:   Matthew 2:1-3

B.2:   Matthew 2: 7f.

C.1:   Of course Herod was troubled. He had every right to be. He was the first man to have ruled the Jews steadily for many years. Herod had brought peace and security.

C.2:   At a price. Herod's spies were everywhere. Herod's bribes were always ready for the informer. Herod's troops were always at hand. Herod's prisons were full. Herod's hands were full of blood.

C.1:   Everyone respected Herod.

M.V.:   We know Herod's type. There are plenty of them in the modern world—plenty of dictators, plenty of tyrants, plenty of secret police.

B.3:   Matthew 2: 11.
Enter the Three Kings with retinue.
Choir sing 249: 'At the name of Jesus' (new tune)

M.V.:   We have few kings today. But we have Presidents, Governors, Chancellors, Prime Ministers, Princes, Heads of State.

B.1:   Psalm 148: 5, 11
Enter a modern politician, likewise to kneel.
Music.
(Kings, etc., fall back into a front row)

B.2:   Matthew 2: 12.

B.3:   Matthew 2: 16.

C.1:   Herod had no real choice. How could he tell what mischief those foreigners were up to? Had there not been plots galore against his life? Did he not live in a sea of intrigue and suspicion?

C.2:   Nobody could trust Herod, that was why there was mistrust all round. Who knew what he would do next, whom he would favour today and destroy tomorrow?

C.1:   Herod was getting old, so naturally he was nervous. Besides, he was ill and in great pain. He knew that he was slowly dying. He still had to keep his kingdom together.

C.2: But how cruel he was! Even the Roman Emperor said that it was better to be Herod's pig than his son. What a tribute!

M.V.: We have bitter experiences like that in the modern world. 'Purges' they are called. It is all part of the struggle for power among ambitious men. Our newspapers are full of it —in politics, in business, in industry.

C.1: Herod believed in the sword. It solved lots of problems.

C.2: But at the cost of making many more. Making bitterness. Making enemies. Causing pain and tears and misery.

C.1: (*imitating Herod*) I order every male child under two years to be killed at once, every child within a day's journey of Bethlehem. I'll teach them who is King in Judaea.

Soldiers enter and march up and down the aisles.

Children sing Hymn 385 (Songs of Praise): 'Unto us a boy is born'

B.1: But Jesus escaped!

B.2: Matthew 2: 13-15a (beginning at Behold, an angel . . .)

(*Enter children again for another dance, shouting 'Jesus escaped'*)

C.1: Herod did not live very long after that. Slowly, painfully, he aged and died. He wanted every prominent Jew taken to the hippodrome and killed at his death, so that there would be real mourning. But it didn't happen.

B.3: Matthew 2: 19-21.

C.2: The struggle for power raged amongst Herod's sons—at least amongst those whom he hadn't murdered. In the end the Romans could stand it no more. They sent their own man to take charge of Judaea. He was called Pontius Pilate.

M.V: It's always happening. Get ride of one oppressor and you only get another. Get rid of one evil, and you get another. Get rid of one war, and you get another, somewhere else. Congo, Angola, Malaysia, Cyprus, Vietnam. So it goes on. Is there no answer?

B.1: We look for a king whom all can trust and obey and love. But thanks be to God! The Christ is come.

B.2: Jesus says 'I, if I be lifted up, will draw all men unto myself'

B.3: Jesus says (reading John 8: 12).

B.1: Jesus says (reading Matthew: 11: 28f).

B.2: Jesus says (reading Matthew 28: 20b).

B.3: Reads Hymn 841, verses 2 and 4.

Minister reads Hymn 861

smallest children come and sing a short carol, then Mary sings Hymn 860 v. 2.

B.1: He is King of kings and Lord of lords.

B.2:   Reads Philippians 2: 10f.

Voices: In America . . . In India . . . In Japan . . . In Rhodesia . . .
         In Germany . . . In China . . . In France . . . In Brazil . . .
         In Russia . . .

M.V: In England. (Pause). In Birkenhead.

B.1:   King of kings and Lord of lords. King supreme.
        All Bible-readers come and kneel before the baby and present
        their Bibles.

Hymn 137, verses 2-4, whilst offering is brought up and presented by
        stewards. Soldiers fall in behind stewards and all kneel
        together.

Minister: Who really is King? (Short speech) Take your choice.
        Jesus or Herod.

Minister: The Benediction

Congregation stand to sing Hymn 143, together, while the lights go
slowly up and the main participants leave first.

Comments

1. A good example of how to make the Incarnation viable in
twentieth century terms. But some will question how much the
word 'king' conveys now? Does it carry the overtones it did in the
days when monarchies were more prevalent? Are the angels credible,
too?

2. The use of different voices is excellent as it brings more variety
in pace and tone. Yet the service is essentially simple and the use of
hymns helps people feel they are in touch with their past experience
as well as trying to worship in a new way.

3. The dramatic content is high and the use of children dancing
breaks up the usual Protestant over-emphasis on words. The style of
writing is terse, easy to follow, with plenty of punch.

4. The service might well be used on the Sunday after Christmas.
The references to the Massacre of the Innocents help to de-senti-
mentalize the Christmas narrative.

Further Comments

1. The service asserts that Jesus reigns, but never indicates *how*
he reigns.

2. Is Herod a good focus? He was only a satellite king at best.
Moreover, the tragedy of his own career and person is not quite
brought out. Wicked men are never totally wicked through and
through, which is why they are so hard to deal with. Thus Herod was
not just a tyrant. He actually had ten wives, but part of his tragedy
was that he had the favourite one murdered because he suspected
her of treason. Afterwards he simply went to pieces.

84

E. A PASSION SERVICE

Source: New Directions, *Spring* 1967

This service, suitable for Palm Sunday, Passion Sunday, or Good Friday, is an extensive adaptation of one submitted by Jack Dowson and Trevor Beeson to the Renewal Group's Ideas Book. But here the Passion story is presented both by symbolism and dramatic reading. The Minister (denoted by M) reads all the narrative portions of Scripture, but all speeches are taken by persons representing Pilate (P), Jesus (J), the High Priest (HP), the Thieves (T), the Messenger (MG), whilst a group sitting in the front row shout for the crowd (CR).

Suggestions for the themes of the prayers are given here. It is precisely in the prayers that the contemporary relevance of the whole drama needs to be brought out. If they can be extempore, so much the better—but in any case, they must be brief and to the point.

The congregation need to have a service sheet which sets out the main stages of the service and gives the hymn numbers, so that no announcements are required. It also needs to set out the following responsive prayer, which is constantly used:

Minister:	O Saviour of the world, who by Thy Cross and precious blood hast redeemed us.
People:	Save us and help us, we humbly beseech Thee, O Lord.
Minister:	Jesus, my Lord, I Thee adore.
People:	O make me love Thee more and more.

A very large candle on a tall stick stands in the centre of the Communion Table, which is otherwise bare.

THE KING ENTERS

M & CR:	Matthew 21: 1-3; 6-11.
Congregation:	Hymn 192: 'Ride on, ride on in majesty' during which P and HP take up places on either side of the Table
Prayer:	A bidding to worship The responsive prayer The Lord's Prayer

THE KING BEFORE THE PRIESTS

M & J:	Matthew 26: 1-4

Enter a messenger, who stands before Pilate.

MG:	Matthew 27: 19.

M, P & CR:	Luke 23: 13-24. Matthew 27: 24-26 during which MG brings a basin to Pilate, who washes his hands in it and places it on the Table
Prayer:	For all of us who attempt to evade our responsibilities: The responsive prayer

THE KING GOES TO CALVARY

M & CR:	Mark 15: 16-19.
Congregation:	Hymn 202 (3 verses): 'O sacred head once wounded' during which a purple robe and a crown of thorns are presented.
M & J:	Luke 23: 26-31
Choir:	Sing 'Take up thy Cross' (tune by Michael Brierley). During this the two thieves carry up large crosses, prop them on opposite sides of the Table, and stand beside them
Prayer:	Forgiveness for our sins The responsive prayer

THE KING CARES

M, J & T:	Luke 23: 39-43.
M:	John 19: 23, 24.
M & J:	John 19: 25-27, after which John moves over to Mary then slowly leads her out
Prayer:	That we care for the heartbroken The responsive prayer
Congregation:	Hymn 182: 'When I survey the wondrous Cross' during which the two thieves leave

THE KING DIES

M & J:	John 19: 28, 29

A crowd member passes a spear to the Minister, who puts it on the Table

M:	Luke 23: 44, 45

All the lights are suddenly put out

M & J:	Luke 23: 46.

The Minister snuffs out the candle, leaving total darkness

M:	Mark 15: 39 and Luke 23: 48. The responsive prayer The Blessing

The Minister drapes the Table with a large black cloth, then the lights go slowly up.

Note

'Take up thy cross' is set to a modern tune in *Thirty 20th Century Hymns* (published by Josef Weinberger, 33 Crawford Street, London W1).

Comments

1. The use of a candle in this and the next order is based on the Roman service of Tenebrae.
2. Should the service end in the death of Christ, just like that?

F. MAUNDY THURSDAY

Source: Rev. J. Rimmer

The service is held in a schoolroom or large hall. Tables are arranged to represent a gathering at a meal. The aim of the service is to share a meal together and to use the materials and symbols of the Last Supper events. The people sit round the tables, as at a meal or wedding reception; the minister takes his place at the head as the host. Announcements and explanation of the order of the service are given at the beginning.

Introduction:	'Behold the Lamb of God' (recording from Handel's 'Messiah')
Hymn 462:	'I hunger and I thirst' (20th Century tune)
Prayer:	*My God, my Glory* (p.71)
Lesson:	John 13: v. 1-5, 12-17
Hymn 564:	'Father I dare believe Thee merciful and true'

Washing of hands ceremony (During the singing of the hymn each person in turn washes the hands of the person next to him by sprinkling water over the fingers over a bowl, then handing the person a hand towel to dry the fingers). If the hymn singing finishes before the washing ceremony, let the hand washing continue in silence. This act becomes an act of confession, of forgiveness and of cleansing.

Prayer: *My God, My Glory* (p.73)

Conversation at the Table

Lessons read by several people sitting round the tables to give the effect of a conversation by the disciples at the Last Supper as they recounted the events in the life of Christ. (John 1: 29-34; Matthew 4: 18-25; Mark 8: 27-31; Mark 8: 34-38; Mark 10: 31-34).

Prayer Meditation: *Secret of the Saints* pp.172-174

Feeding on Christ: Mark 14: 12-25

Prayer: Words of Institution: *My God, My Glory*
                          (p.70)

Distribution of bread and wine (One large cottage loaf is used and
at the Words of Institution broken in half. Now each half is passed
round the sitting people. Each serves the other and says 'Peace be
unto you' as the loaf is passed to the next person to take a piece off
and eat. Likewise the cup or tray of individual glasses is passed round
from one person to the next in silence. Each serves the other and is
served by the person next to him).

Prayer: *My God, My glory* (p.82)

Hymn 768:   'O Bread to pilgrims given'
    (During this hymn the lights are dimmed in the hall)

Candles of failure ceremony:
    Candles are placed on the tables (and had been lit before the
service started) to represent the light of the disciples and Christ
Himself as the darkness of the cross approaches. Each candle is put
out in turn and a verse recited to indicate the failure of the disciples
and the death of Christ.

'We put out the first candle, remembering how Peter three times
denied that he knew Jesus' (Put out candle)
        Peter, vexed and tired, thrice denied his own master,
        Said he never knew him—to stop a girl's clack.
        O Lord have mercy. Lighten our darkness.
        We have all denied you and our light is black.

'We put out the second candle, remembering how Judas betrayed
Jesus' (Put out candle)
        Judas loved his pride and rejected his master.
        Judas turned traitor and lost his way back.
        O Lord have mercy. Lighten our darkness.
        We have all been traitors and our light is black.

'We put out the third candle, remembering how all the disciples for-
sook Jesus and fled' (Put out candle)
        Twelve all ran away and forsook their dear master
        Left him lonely prisoner, a lamb in wolves' pack.
        O Lord have mercy. Lighten our darkness.
        We have crucified you and our light is black.

'We put out the fourth candle, remembering how the crowd shouted
"Crucify" ' (Put out candle)
        Pilate asked the crowd to release the good master.
        'Crucify,' they shouted, 'We don't want him back.'
        O Lord have mercy. Lighten our darkness
        We have crucified you and our light is black.

'We put out the last candle, remembering how all of us by our sins have denied and betrayed Jesus' (Put out candle)

> We have watched the crowd and scoffed at the master
> Thought we knew much better and tried our own tack.
> O Lord, have mercy. Lighten our darkness.
> We have all reviled you and our light is black.

(One candle is relit) Christ's light shines on.

Hymn 180:   'There is a green hill'
               'After they had sung a hymn, they went out . . .'
               Benediction

ALTERNATIVE MAUNDY THURSDAY SERVICE

Arrangements as before but after the 'Washing of hands' ceremony, a simple meal of fish and bread is served by the host to each member (just a small portion that is easily eaten with the fingers) as a symbol of the idea that to eat with someone is to have forgiven from the heart. The fish and bread also link with the Resurrection meal Jesus had with His disciples. After the meal comes the 'Conversation at the Table', Bread and Wine, and the Candle of Failures Ceremony.

Notes

My God, My Glory by Eric Milner-White is published by SPCK.
Secret of the Saints by Henry Lunn was published by Heffers of Cambridge in 1933. If unavailable it should not be hard to find a suitable reading from some other source.

Comments

1. An unusual service for Maundy Thursday, appropriately sober. There is a good use of symbolism and an intelligent use of the late Dean of York's prayers (*My God, My Glory*). The fish and bread symbolism points back to the historical roots of the Christian faith, linking this act with acts in the past, but needs careful presentation.

2. Does the act of *hand-washing* adequately represent the *feet-washing* of Jesus? It could represent something else equally prominent in the Passion narrative. Hand-washing in the post-Freud era has very different connotations! Can we not find other hymns than 'There is a green hill far away' with its picture of a pale Galilean?

Further Comments

1. This service would leave one asking the somewhat legalistic question of whether the Lord's Supper has been celebrated or not.

2. Traditionally, at least, the relighting of a candle does not symbolize Christ's continuing faithfulness (which would require a symbol that is not extinguished at all) but the Resurrection. It should therefore come at the very end of the service.

G. EASTER DAWN VIGIL

Source: Rev. Norwyn Denny

(5 a.m. Easter morning—outside the church)

Gospel for the day: John 20: 1-10.

Hymn 205:   'Jesus Christ is risen today'

Epistle: 1 Corinthians 15: 20-28 and 50-58 or Colossians 3: 1-7

Hymn 216:   'Jesus lives'

M: 'Jesus says . . .
Here I stand knocking at the door; if anyone hears my voice and opens the door, I will come in and sit down to supper (breakfast) with him and he with me. To him who is victorious I will grant a place on my throne, as I myself was victorious and sat down with my Father on his throne.'
Knocking and Opening of the doors of the Church

Prayers:

M: (Facing open door of church)
Thanks be to thee, O Christ, because thou hast broken for us the bonds of sin and brought us into fellowship with the Father

P: AMEN

M: Thanks be to thee, O Christ, because thou hast overcome death and opened to us the gate of eternal life

P: AMEN

M: Thanks be to thee, O Christ, because where two or three are gathered in thy name there thou art in the midst of them

P: AMEN

M: Thanks be to thee, O Christ, because thou ever livest to make intercession for us

P: AMEN

M: For these and all other benefits of thy mighty resurrection, thanks be unto thee, O Christ

P: AMEN

All: The Lord's Prayer
(Inside the porch of the church, the candles which were all extinguished on Maundy Thursday are relit, and carried into the church by seven people to be placed on the stand together)

M: Let us pray: May the Light of the glorious and risen Christ banish all darkness from our hearts and minds.

M: The Lord be with you

P: And with thy spirit.

M: Bless, we beseech thee, O God, the light we bring; and grant that all we who this morning will be sharers in the Sacrament of thy presence, may be fulfilled with thy grace and heavenly benediction, that as we were sometime in darkness, but now are light in the Lord, we may walk as children of light; through the same our Lord Jesus Christ, Amen.

All: Sing Hymn 204 as they enter the church.

Comments

1. A further service from Notting Hill, but the language is still that of the traditionalists. However, the use of movement and light is introduced to amplify the Easter story in its traditional form.

2. Some will be glad to realize that Christians can worship out of doors, but should Christians end up on Easter Day entering church (even for communion)? Can a similar exit be devised?

Further Comments

This is useful if it is not confused with the great Easter Vigil of tradition. This service here is based on the Roman service of lighting the Paschal candle, which has some fine material just after this point which would be useful to supplement what is here.

5. Special Occasions and Themes

INTRODUCTION

THESE OCCASIONS usually present the Church with an excellent opportunity to relate its life to the world. The situations themselves provide an occasion for secular worship, worship that grows out of a secular occasion where people who are normally outside the Church are involved with those who are members. An obvious instance is that of a stone-laying, where builders and congregation are brought together by the mutual interest of erecting the church. This should be more than a formal occasion in which the processes of building and the builders are ignored, but a chance for the church to understand something of what goes into the making of the building they are to use, and for the builders to have an insight into the purpose that lies behind the work they are doing.

For the Church, then, it is all important that the occasion should be studied thoroughly, all the issues involved considered, and every chance taken to learn from it. This is an obvious instance when the Church should listen to what God is saying to it through the world. So in the service on 'God and Politics' it is the people involved in Local Government who speak, and the Church which listens. Both gain, for the one who speaks gains new insights about his own vocation by having to think of it in the context of the worshipping community.

It is important, therefore, to consider what will enable those people (some of whom may not attend Church often) to share in the service fully. Traditional elements are necessary, since familiarity will give assurance. But there should also be elements which will, by their relevance and pertinence, provoke and disturb. The Church and the secular world will not always find it comfortable to meet. However, there should be basic appreciation and sympathy, without which provocation will merely irritate and confirm misunderstanding.

In such worship the immense richness of the secular world provides evidence of the goodness of God, and should prevent thanksgiving from becoming vague and formal. The concerns of the world should come home in their urgency and make confession and intercession real. By its meeting with the secular, the worshipping congregation is called out from concerns about itself to its true mission to serve the world. Too often special occasions are thought of as times when the Church can advertise itself, enlisting the support and seeking the approbation of the world. It should be seen much more as a chance for the Church to learn from the world what God's will is for it, and to establish a real relationship with the world. Then worship becomes a true means of unity and communication, under the God who is the Lord of all life.

A. LAYING THE FOUNDATION STONE OF A CHURCH

Source: Rev. Colin Groom

THE LAYING OF THE STONE
Everyone is asked to assemble on the site of the new church

M: Our help is in the name of the Lord
P: who made heaven and earth

M: Unless the Lord builds the house
P: in vain do its builders labour.

M: Give praise to the Father Almighty;
P: To His Son, Jesus Christ the Lord;
M: To the Spirit who dwells in our hearts;
P: Both now and for ever. Amen.

M: O Lord God, Maker of all worlds, You have taught us that You seek to live and move among us, and that we ourselves are Your temple. We therefore ask You in Your abundant goodness to come among us here, as we erect these walls to house Your living temple; through Jesus Christ our Lord.
P: Amen.

M: Go before us, O Lord, in all our doings with Your most gracious favour, and further us with Your continual help; that in all our works, begun, continued, and ended in You, we may glorify Your holy name, and finally by Your mercy obtain everlasting life; through Jesus Christ our Lord.
P: Amen.

HYMN (tune: Gersau):
> 1. Thou, who hast in Zion laid
>   The true foundation-stone,
>   And with those a covenant made
>   Who build on that alone:
>   Hear us, Architect divine,
>   Great Builder of Thy church below!
>   Now upon Thy servants shine,
>   Who seek Thy praise to show.

2. Earth is Thine; her thousand hills
    Thy mighty hand sustains;
Heaven Thy awful presence fills;
    O'er all Thy glory reigns:
Yet the place of old prepared
    By regal David's favoured son
Thy peculiar blessing shared,
    And stood Thy chosen throne.

3. We, like Jesse's son, would raise
    A temple to the Lord:
Sound throughout its courts His praise,
    His saving name record:
Dedicate a house to Him,
    Who, once in mortal weakness shrined,
Sorrowed, suffered, to redeem,
    To rescue all mankind.

4. Father, Son, and Spirit, send
    The consecrating flame;
Now in majesty descend,
    Inscribe the living name;
That great name by which we live
    Now write on this accepted stone;
Us into Thy hands receive,
    Our temple make Thy throne.

M: As St. Paul reminds us, 'There can be no other foundation beyond that which is laid; I mean Jesus Christ Himself.'

Introduction of stone-layer, who, with the builder's assistance, will then lay the stone in its place, with the words

'TO THE GLORY OF GOD I LAY THIS STONE'

M: In this place may the true faith flourish, the honouring of God, the love of the brethren; here may the voice of prayer continually be heard, the voice of rejoicing and thankfulness, the voice of the weak and perplexed, the voice of those who look for peace and justice, the voice of little children, the voice of those who in all things call on the name of the Father, the Son, and the Holy Spirit.

P: Amen.

M: Almighty and everlasting God, we believe that You have put it into our hearts to erect this building for the service of Your people. Grant us then, O Lord, Your presence here; protect and help those who are working to erect this building; grant that it may soon stand complete in strength and beauty, and

that all those who have worked to see this building erected
may themselves be built up in love; through Jesus Christ our
Lord.

P: Amen.

All: Our Father . . .

M: The Lord be with you
P: And with you also

At this point, everyone is asked to proceed into the existing church
hall

THE WORD OF GOD
HYMN 685: 'Stand up and bless the Lord'

First Lesson, read by the Secretary of the Baptist Church

Second Lesson, read by the Vicar

HYMN (tune: 'Regent Square' or 'Westminster Abbey')

1 Christ is made the sure foundation,
    Christ the head and corner-stone.
Chosen of the Lord, and precious,
Binding all the Church in one
Holy Sion's help for ever,
    And her confidence alone.

2 To this temple, where we call Thee,
    Come, O Lord of hosts, today;
With Thy wanted loving-kindness
    Hear Thy servants as they pray;
And Thy fullest benediction
    Shed within its walls alway.

3 Here vouchsafe to all Thy servants
    What they ask of Thee to gain,
What they gain from Thee for ever
    With the blessed to retain.
And hereafter in Thy glory
    Evermore with Thee to reign.

4 Laud and honour to the Father,
    Laud and honour to the Son,
Laud and honour to the Spirit,
    Ever Three and ever One;
One in might, and One in glory,
    While unending ages run.

SERMON

OUR OFFERING
of Belief

  Minister and people stand and say: The Apostles' Creed.

of Money

  A collection will be made, and this offering will be dedicated
along with the contents of the Building Fund gift boxes

of Prayer

  A member of the uniting churches will make suggestions for
prayer. After each suggestion, there will be this response:

    Leader: In your mercy, O Lord,
    People: Hear our prayer

CONCLUSION

The Notices

HYMN 703: 'City of God, how broad and far'

THE BLESSING

Comments

1. The complications of a building site may not allow elaborate
worship and the simplicity of this service is apt, but it is a pity that
the service moves into a hall. Instead of a sermon, which is seldom
suitable for the open air, the features of the site could have been
exploited and the builders incorporated into the worship. Here
church members, builders, and the public are brought together by
the situation and there is an opportunity to express a common
purpose. The act of stone-laying is passed over rather quickly
without any suggestion of its significance; as an act of faith and hope;
as a witness to the faith; as a contribution to the welfare of the
community. The act and significance of the building of a church does
not seem to have been fully considered:

    If you are going to build a church
     you are going to create a thing which speaks.
    It will speak of meanings and of values,
     and it will go on speaking.
    And if it speaks of the wrong values
     it will go on destroying.
    There is a responsibility here.[1]

2. There is more interest in the purposes for which the building is
to be used than the sacramental nature of the building itself. Unless

[1] Peter Hammond, *Towards a Church Architecture* (Architectural Press).

96

there is this appreciation of the value of the work in process, of all that it means to those involved and the community it is to serve, it does not seem necessary to celebrate a stone-laying. But in the work itself there is such rich expression of the relation of the Church to the community that this should be made an opportunity for the Church and world to celebrate the Lord of all the activities and hopes of man. To retreat into a hall suggests withdrawal from the world (a sad characteristic of nonconformity).

3. It would help in a situation like this to explore Biblical references to such occasions (e.g. Ezra 3), not so much to use them as to find out what the Bible considered appropriate at such times.

4. 'You' is used consistently throughout, though this conflicts with the usage of the hymns—a perennial problem for reformers of liturgical language! It is a mistake to pray, as in two of the prayers here, for God to come among us. Surely He is here and what is needed is for us to have eyes to recognize His presence.

Further Comments

1. 'City of God, how broad and far' is a very nebulous hymn, and for 'Christ is made the sure foundation' there are better tunes than 'Regent Square', notably 'Westminster Abbey'.

2. The service has a good structure, but is not very imaginative. Some of the language is but traditionalism turned into 'you'.

3. The commentary above expresses disapproval (not for the first time) of praying to God to come among us. Surely He was there before the Incarnation, yet surely He 'came' in Christ and comes in Word and Sacrament. This emphasis on 'recognizing' His presence ignores the 'scandal of particularity'.

B. THANKSGIVING AND DEDICATION FOR A NEW CHURCH

Source: Rev. C. Hughes Smith

The congregation will be in their places and the door will be locked at 2.55 p.m. The ministers will proceed from the Vestry to the Door of the Church at 3 p.m. At the Door, the Superintendent Minister will say:

Go before us, O Lord, in all our doings with thy most gracious favour, and further us with thy continual help; that in all our works begun, continued, and ended in thee, we may glorify thy holy name, and finally by thy mercy obtain everlasting life;

through Jesus Christ our Lord. Amen.

The Superintendent will then knock on the Door, which will be opened from within by the Senior Society Steward, who will say:

The Church is assembled. Will you lead us in thanksgiving and worship and dedication in our new home?

The Steward will lead the ministers to their places

The Superintendent Minister will announce the hymn

HYMN 2:'All people that on earth do dwell'

The Lord's Prayer

THANKSGIVING

Minister:	Thanks be to thee, most glorious God, Father, Son and Holy Spirit, for making thyself known to mankind, for the power of the gospel of Christ, and for the life of the people of God:
People:	Thanks be to thee, O Lord
Minister:	For those who have preached the gospel and those who have shown in their lives the fruit of the Spirit:
People:	Thanks be to thee, O Lord
Minister:	For those who by planning and giving and building have completed this house to the glory of God:
People:	Thanks be to thee, O Lord
Minister:	For our friends who serve Christ in other parts of the world, and for those in the other world, who, serving him still, rejoice with us today:
People:	Thanks be to thee, O Lord
Minister:	We beseech thee to equip thy people with thy Spirit for work in thy service:
People:	We beseech thee to hear us
Minister:	That it may please thee to bless the whole world through thy people in this place:
People:	We beseech thee to hear us
Minister:	That Christ may be set forth as evidently crucified before men's eyes:
People:	We beseech thee to hear us
Minister:	That thy people here may be sensitive to the needs of the neighbourhood and eager to serve in the Spirit of love:
People:	We beseech thee to hear us

The Minister will conclude the Thanksgiving by prayer on behalf of the congregation

A description of events leading up to the building of the new church

THE MINISTRY OF THE WORD

Prayer at the Pulpit: (The Superintendent Minister)	Grant, O Lord, that the word of life may here be proclaimed with faithfulness and power. May the preachers of the word be filled with thy Spirit; may the hearers of the word act upon it; and may preacher and people together truly serve thy kingdom. through Jesus Christ our Lord. Amen.
Reading from the Old Testament	Genesis 28: 10-19 read by a member of Family Church
HYMN 702:	'Christ is our corner-stone'
Reading from the New Testament Anthem:	Ephesians 2: 11-22. read by a Local Preacher. 'I was glad when they said unto me,' Richard Graves
The Sermon	The Chairman of the District
The Gloria	Glory be to God on high. . . .

THE DEDICATION

The congregation will sing the verses of the hymn and the ministers will lead the prayers:

> Jesu, thou Joy of loving hearts,
> > Thou Fount of life, thou Light of men,
> From the best bliss that earth imparts
> > We turn unfilled to thee again.

> Thy truth unchanged hath ever stood,
> > Thou savest those that on thee call;
> To them that seek thee thou art good,
> > To them that find thee, all in all.

Prayer at the Font:	Almighty God, our heavenly Father, without whom no word or work of ours availeth, we thank thee for the sacrament of baptism, whereby we are privileged to share in the life of thy Son. Grant that those who shall be baptized here may receive thy Holy Spirit, and belonging to thy Church, may rejoice in their salvation and fulfil their calling in mission and service. And let this font ever witness, in the hearts of all who worship here, to the covenant which thou hast made with them; through Jesus Christ our Lord. Amen.

We taste thee, O thou living Bread,
And long to feast upon thee still;
We drink of thee, the Fountain-head
And thirst our souls from thee to fill.

Prayer at the
Communion Table:

Almighty God, give ear to the prayers which we humbly present before thee. We render thanks to thee for the remembrance of the passion and resurrection of thy Son, and we beseech thee to grant that the offering made upon this table may be acceptable and pleasing to thee; that thy blessed Son may be made known in the breaking of the bread, his presence thankfully acknowledged by faithful hearts, and his death constantly proclaimed until he come;

through Jesus Christ our Lord. Amen.

Our restless spirits yearn for thee;
Where'er our changeful lot is cast;
Glad when thy gracious smile we see,
Blest when our faith can hold thee fast.

Prayer in the
Church hall:

Almighty God, who hast called thy people into existence for thy glory and for the blessing of the whole world, use this place, we beseech thee, to build up thy people in love. May the life of thy family be rich in skill and wisdom; may the activities we undertake explore the ways of thy Spirit and the goodness of thy creation, and may one generation here declare thy works to another,

through Jesus Christ our Lord. Amen.

O Jesus, ever with us stay:
Make all our moments calm and bright;
Chase the dark night of sin away;
Shed o'er the world thy holy light.
Amen.

Prayer of
Dedication
said together

O eternal God, whom the heaven of heavens cannot contain, much less these walls made with hands, who yet hast promised thy presence where two or three are gathered in thy name, we beseech thee to hallow this building which we now solemnly dedicate to thee, Father, Son, and Holy Spirit. We name it to be thy house, the place where thy people gather to worship thee in spirit and in truth,

where thou dost speak in mercy and judgement, and where they are renewed by thine
inexhaustible grace, who livest and reignest,
Three Persons in One God, world without
end, Amen.

THE OFFERING

Declaration, by the Chairman of the District	We declare that this place is dedicated for the service of God in the world and for his people's worship. May all who gather listen faithfully to God's holy word, and offer spiritual sacrifices acceptable to him. May they never be ashamed to confess the faith of Christ crucified and risen from the dead, but strengthened by his Body and Blood, may they in every part of the world be his faithful servants unto their lives' end.
Congregation:	Amen. Thanks be to God.

THE DOXOLOGY
will be sung

HYMN 386: 'O Thou who camest from above'

BENEDICTION

You are warmly invited to have tea after the Service.

At 7.30 tonight, there will be a production in the church of *The Boy
with the Cart* by Christopher Fry.

THE DEDICATION OF THE CHURCH BUILDING will be completed by the
Sacrament of Holy Communion at 8 o'clock tomorrow morning,
Sunday, and by the Sacrament of Holy Baptism during Family
Worship at 11 o'clock.

Comments

1. This order owes much to the *Church of South India Book of
Common Worship; Supplement, Part I* (Oxford). There is drama and a
sense of celebration about this service which suits the occasion. The
opening worship is especially fine.

2. There is a sound understanding of what constitutes dedication.
Pronouncing holy words over an object or place is a pagan survival
associated with exorcism. Christian dedication is through thanksgiving and use. It is through the *use* of the buildings and furnishings
that they are set apart for their special functions. Therefore the
announcements at the end of this service are an integral part of the
act of worship. It might be difficult, though not impossible, to use the
font for a baptism there and then, just as the pulpit is used for the

Ministry of the Word during the service; but there seems to be no good reason why the communion table could not be dedicated by the celebration of Holy Communion. Doesn't this reflect our Methodist preference for the word rather than the sacraments?

3. As with the previous service there is little or no reference to the builders or architect, whereas this is an excellent opportunity for them to take part in the service. The emphasis is much more on the benefits the congregation will receive from the Church than upon the mission of the church as the servant of the Community.

4. The ending does not maintain the strength of the opening. It would have been better if the whole congregation and not just the chairman made the final declaration of dedication. In fact, the service is far too much of a parson's performance. The language of the service is simple and dignified, and the use of the hymn with prayers of dedication interspersed is especially fitting.

Further Comments

This is a satisfying service with a splendid beginning. The use of a hymn as a response might be ragged and 'Hereford', as in the Baptist Church Hymnary, would be a more appropriate tune than 'Wareham'.

C. GOD AND POLITICS

Source: Rev. Richard Jones

A special service for Christian Citizenship Sunday in which we are privileged to welcome

His Worship the Mayor,

The Councillor for Mersey Ward,

The Councillor for Claughton Ward and the Chairman, Liberal Party National Executive,

The Councillor for Prenton ward.

Introit

Minister: Christ is the supreme authority in the whole universe. All political power is a grant from Him. Hear what St. Paul declares . . . (reading Ephesians 1: 20).

Prayer: That we shall hear God's Word through this worship

Hymn 271: 'Crown Him with many crowns'

Lesson: Psalm 21: 1-7   the Minister
Romans 13: 1-10   His Worship the Mayor

Hymn 811: 'Thy kingdom come, O God'

The Christian in National Politics—A Councillor

Prayer: Confession for our nation's sins

Hymn 883: 'Judge eternal, throned in splendour'
Politics does good for human welfare—A Councillor

Prayer: Thanksgiving for the welfare agencies
Problems for Christians in politics and the need for greater Christian involvement—A Councillor

Hymn 615: 'Guide me, O thou great Jehovah'
(during this hymn the offertory will be received. We remain standing at the close)

Prayers: For politicians and the strengths they need
For development in our town and better housing
For Christians to enter politics
For ourselves—to love our neighbour

Silence

A creed for politics (to be said together): I believe in Jesus Christ, King of kings and Lord of lords. I believe that I must obey His will, love my neighbour for Christ's sake, seek the welfare of all mankind. I believe Christ wants politics to do these things. I pledge myself to this purpose, now and ever. So help me, God. Amen.

The Lord's Prayer

Hymn 272: 'Jesus shall reign'

BENEDICTION

Comments

1. An excellent service for Christian Citizenship Sunday since it is those representing society who speak and generally determine the pattern of the service. Rightly the minister does not preach, since at a time like this the church should listen to society. The movement of the service reflects Charles Peguy's saying that:

'Everything begins in mysticism and ends in politics.'

2. It moves from affirmations about Christ to practical issues. Prayers grow out of the addresses and follow the liturgical pattern of confession, thanksgiving, and intercession. A form of Creed at the end affirms Christian conviction about society. It does not attempt to restate the articles of the Apostles' or Nicene Creeds, but concentrates on a specific area of conviction and concern. This prevents the creed from becoming unreal for such a mixed congregation as this.

Further Comments

1. What would Amos have made of the first comment above?

2. What would the New Testament writers have made of the second comment above? A mixed congregation in this post-Christen-

dom era raises problems about worship in general and Creeds in particular. The solution in the service is perhaps to be commended, but the above comment seems to suggest that a 'mixed' congregation should have no difficulty about affirming 'Christian conviction about society', as if that were somehow easier than saying the Apostles' Creed. It is true that all men of good will may believe that they must 'seek the welfare of all mankind', but the words 'I believe in Jesus Christ' must be given their full meaning and might be a 'skandalon' to those who are not professing Christians.

D. A SERVICE OF THANKSGIVING FOR AGRICULTURE, INDUSTRY, AND COMMERCE

Source: Rev. Michael Appleyard, Salisbury, Rhodesia

CALL TO WORSHIP

Minister: Let us worship God.

Hymn 28: 'All creatures of our God and King' (five verses)

AN ACT OF PRAISE:

Minister: Let us pray.
O God our Father,
We praise you because we see you are the creator of this universe—in the life-giving sun by day, in the moon by night, the galaxies of stars, the immensities of space, in the beauty of nature and the marvels of energy

People: We acknowledge you and praise you as the Lord of all creation

Minister: We praise you because we see you in the development of men, the growth of nations and the movements of peoples

People: We acknowledge you and praise you as the Lord of all history

Minister: We praise you because we see you leading people to discover the meaning and purpose of life

People: We acknowledge you and praise you as the Lord of truth and life

Minister: We praise you because we see you at work as men and women put to good use the raw material of creation; experiment, plant, and build; manufacture, produce and use all that is entrusted to us

People: We acknowledge you and praise you as the Lord of agriculture and mining, industry and commerce, science and technology.

Minister: We praise you because we see you incarnate and revealed in Jesus, the carpenter of Nazareth, in whom all work is made sacred

People: We acknowledge you and praise you as the Lord of all work

Minister: We praise you because we see you cooperating with men in their work, seeking to make things of true value, reconciling differences between management and workers, and bringing peace to the world of industry

People: We acknowledge you and praise you as the Lord of reconciliation

Minister: We praise you because we see you helping people to contact one another and transport to one another the products of man's work

People: We acknowledge you and praise you as the Lord of communications and trade

Minister: We praise you because we see condemned on the Cross on which Jesus was killed, selfishness, pride, the avoidance of responsibility, hard-heartedness and cowardice; and see exalted as the one hope of all, the love that seeks to save and be spent in the service of others, the love that sacrifices, the love that unites and the love that conquers

People: We acknowledge you and praise you as the source and Lord of love.

Hymn (Tune: Spanish Chant).
1 God of concrete, God of steel,
   God of piston and of wheel,
   God of pylon, God of steam,
   God of girder and of beam,
   God of atom, God of mine,
       All the world of power is Thine!

2 Lord of cable, Lord of rail,
   Lord of motorway and mail,
   Lord of rocket, Lord of flight,
   Lord of soaring satellite,
   Lord of lightning's livid line
       All the world of speed is Thine!

3 God of Turk and God of Greek,
    God of every tongue men speak,
God of Arab, God of Jew,
    God of every racial hue,
God of Laos and Palestine
    All the world of men is Thine!

4 Lord of science, Lord of art,
    Lord of map and graph and chart,
Lord of physics and research,
    Word of Bible, Faith of Church,
Lord of sequence and design,
    All the world of truth is Thine.

5 God whose glory fills the earth,
    Gave the universe its birth,
Loosed the Christ with Easter's might,
    Saves the world from evil's blight,
Claims mankind by grace divine,
    All the world of love is Thine!

(R. G. Jones)

BIBLE READING FROM THE OLD TESTAMENT:
The first reading is from the Book of Deuteronomy chapter 26, verses 1-4, and 17-18.

The people are commanded to offer the first fruits of the land to God as an acknowledgement that the land is his gift to man, and also to walk in his ways and obey his voice.

AN ACT OF CONFESSION, RENUNCIATION, AFFIRMATION, AND SUPPLICATION:

Confession

Minister: When he was asked, 'Which commandment is first of of all?' Jesus answered: 'The first is, Hear, O Israel: the Lord your God is the only Lord; love the Lord your God with all you heart, with all your soul, with all your mind, and with all your strength. The second is this: Love your neighbour as yourself. There is no other commandment greater than these.'

To the God who loves us and who is ready to forgive us, let us pray.

Minister and People: Father, not one of us has clean hands and a pure heart. We have neither loved you nor our neighbour in the ways we ought. We have resisted recognizing you as the Lord of every part of our lives and the Lord of all life. Forgive us as we turn to you again.

106

Minister: If our turning to God for forgiveness is to be creative, let us renounce those things which make us sin, and affirm the things which help us to be strong and faithful to the Lord.

Renunciation
Minister: Are you willing to renounce all self-centredness in speech and action, all self-seeking and self-satisfaction?
People: We are, in the power of the Lord.

Minister: Are you willing to renounce all superficiality, the too easy acceptance of the opinions of others and the avoidance of the careful search for the truth?
People: We are, in the power of the Lord.

Affirmation
Minister: Will you, therefore, leave self behind and follow Jesus in his love and care for the people of every kind?
People: We will, in the power of the Lord.

Minister: Will you commit yourselves to the service of God and your fellow-men of whatever income-bracket, colour or religion, happy and content that this is God's will for you?
People: We will, in the power of the Lord.

Supplication
Minister: Grant us, Father, the power to renounce what we know to be wrong or selfish, and enable us to follow the leading of your Spirit in all our relationships and dealings with other people.
People: Grant this, we pray.

Minister: Grant us, Father, a deeper insight into your great love for this world and its people, revealed to us in the birth, life, death, and resurrection of Jesus Christ.
People: Grant this, we pray.

Minister: Grant, O Father, that we may grow in love so that our love may become like yours.
People: Grant this, we pray

Minister: For the sake of Jesus Christ
People: Amen.

All: The Lord's Prayer.

BIBLE READING FROM THE NEW TESTAMENT

The second reading is from Paul's letter to the Colossians, chapter 1, verses 15-20

HYMN (Tune composed for this Service)

1 O God, who made metal, steam and fire,
And taught us to fashion from our desire,
The ways and means of using them,
We bring you a harvest reaped from skill,
We who are town and city men.

2 O God, who made the sky and ocean,
And taught us the laws of speed and motion
That we might better conquer them,

3 O God, who made sound and light and heat,
And taught us how we might complete,
The miracle by using them.

4 O God, who made colour, tone and hue,
And taught us how we might construe,
A greater depth in using them.

5 O God, who made brick and stone and clay,
And taught us how we might display,
Our love for you in fashioning them,
                              Mrs Jennifer Lafitte
                              (written for this service)

AN ACT OF DEDICATION AND INTERCESSION

Leader: We are now assembled for the purpose of dedicating soil that is cultivated, seed that is planted, tools that are used on the land, machines from the factory, the equipment of the office and the workers that labour in the service of God and for the good of all.

1st Speaker: Soil we bring to you, O Lord.

Leader: May the Lord teach us to use and conserve this soil and increase its fertility year by year.

2nd Speaker: Seed we bring to you, O Lord.

Leader: May the Lord bless this seed, and cause it to bring forth food for the men, women, and children in our society.

3rd Speaker: Our tools and machines we lay at your feet, O Lord.

Leader: May the Lord strengthen us to use these implements—the hoe, the badza, the plough, the tractor, and also the machines in our factories which grind and bake, process and can our daily food.

4th Speaker:	Our typewriters and ledgers we offer to you, O Lord.
Leader:	May the Lord help you to plan, account, and record, and do your business honestly, accurately, and justly.
Group of Speakers:	We come to you, O Lord, as representatives of the workers of this world—farmers, machine operators, drivers, clerks, accountants, and executives—and dedicate ourselves and our work to you.
Leader:	May the Lord bless you as you work with him, whatever your work may be. Acknowledge your responsibilities; cultivate the soil with care using compost and fertilizers to replace the goodness, save it from erosion or being wasted by weeds; handle your tools and machines with respect and keep them serviced; drive with care and courtesy and deliver your loads; let integrity, right relationships, and an understanding of one another's problems and needs seal all your duties.

Let us pray

That men and women may increasingly work together for the good of all and for the welfare of the community.

That the rich resources of the earth may be used to do away with hunger and malnutrition and bring health and strength to all people.

That towns and cities, as well as farmland and bush, may be places of beauty and free from ugliness, squalor and disease.

That God will accept the offering of the world of agriculture, industry, and commerce, and help us to work with him

Through Jesus Christ our Lord

ALL:	Amen
HYMN 35:	'For the beauty of the earth'
ADDRESS	
HYMN 604:	'Fill Thou my life'
BLESSING	
Minister:	Go forth into the world in peace: be of good courage: hold fast that which is good: render to no man evil for evil: strengthen the fainthearted: support the weak: help the afflicted: honour all men: love and serve the Lord, rejoicing in the

power of the Holy Spirit. And the blessing of God Almighty, the Father, the Son and the Holy Spirit, be upon you, and remain with you for ever. Amen.

Note:

This service was compiled by the Sub-Committee for Worship and Evangelism of the Salisbury Council of Churches, Rhodesia, and was a Sunday afternoon act of Thanksgiving on the occasion of the 7th Royal Salisbury Show in 1964. The singing was led by a Salvation Army Band.

The service was printed and somehow conducted both in English and Shona, and must have been a significant act of united praise on the part of the two main racial groups.

Comments

1. This is a united act of witness that stresses the social concern of the Church. It took place under difficult circumstances where such united worship provoked critical comment and a certain amount of tension. In itself the service is not provocative, but it deals with spheres of life where there must have been tensions. Rightly in such circumstances it does not dwell on problems (there is, for instance, no clear confession of the evils which accompany our industrial society) but on the goodness of God and the responsibility of man as the agent of God. It deals with the concerns and the issues of the three spheres of labour, mentioning the instruments involved as symbols. The language is clear and down to earth, avoiding traditional clichés.

2. That God is the Lord of all life is made clear in the prayers and hymns, though in some places the arguing of a case makes the concepts rather strained; for example:

Minister: We praise you because we see you helping people to contact one another, and transport to one another the products of man's work.

This conjures up an interesting, but distracting picture of God as an agent of communications and transport. Prayers, and especially responsive prayers, should be simple and direct rather than discursive.

3. The order of the service follows an interesting pattern. After an opening act of praise there is an Old Testament exhortation which leads to confession, which then takes the form of renunciation, affirmation, and supplication. This may be a weakness, since no sin is confessed. These would seem to be spheres of life where confession was necessary, but under the circumstances in which the service was carried out confession may have been interpreted as provocation. The Gospel follows and then the dedication of talents, of the earth,

110

and of implements, with intercessions. The address (as so often in such services) comes late in the service, divorced from the ministry of the word where it properly belongs. It would have strengthened the service if the intercession and dedication had come at the end before the sending of the congregation out into the world.

Further Comments

1. Perhaps it is inevitable that a service which is about agriculture should be stronger on creation than redemption.

2. It is not desirable to have one of the main items in between the Old and New Testament readings.

3. The language is too discursive and sometimes submits to jargon (e.g. 'income-bracket').

E. OUR LORD AND OUR TEACHING

Source: Rev. Frank Godfrey

'If it is teaching, let us give all that we have to our teaching'
(Romans 12: 7, J. B. Phillips version.)

M: Jesus said 'whoever among you wants to be great, must become the servant of you all: for the Son of Man Himself has not come to be served, but to serve'

P: Our purpose is not to become the God of the classroom
Nor to make our class the pride of the school
Nor to make our school the showcase of the city.
We serve the child, because he will become a man.
Because his mind and Spirit are hungry
We shall feed him.

M: Jesus said 'I am come that they may have life'

P: We teach for their sake, that they may know God's world
Knowing, that they may delight and worship in it
Delighting, that their lives may find free service and expression in it

M: Jesus was born in a borrowed crib, accepted friendship from disciples, ointment from Mary, and the Cross from His enemies. All these He touched with a new glory.

P: Our selves and our gifts we offer for His service, in teaching.
We do not want to be envious of the talents of a colleague
But to be glad of our own gifts.
Accept and glorify our gifts, O Lord.

M: Jesus said that happiness belonged to the humble-minded, the meek, the merciful, the sincere, those hungry and thirsty for goodness.

111

8

P: Let us share this happiness.
We shall reassess ourselves and our work, and be ready to alter what is wrong.
We shall be prepared to learn from the experience and character of other people.
We shall co-operate freely with those in authority over us, Headmasters, or heads of departments, remembering the particular responsibilities they always bear.
When we are in authority, we shall have the grace to be open to advice and, if necessary, correction, from those under us.

M: Jesus had all things committed to Him from the Father, but yet wrapped Himself, took a towel and washed the feet of the disciples.

P: Help us O Lord to accept the mundane things that sometimes gall our spirits, as part of our total education in living together: the milk and the bank; duties in lunchtime or break; extra work for a sick colleague or a student teacher; the visit of inspectors and health workers.

M: Jesus welcomed children with their mothers and blessed them. He said 'Let them come, for of such is the Kingdom.'

P: Grant that we might share your compassion, Lord, and therefore your patience with awkward children or fussy parents.

M: Jesus said 'My peace I give you'.

P: Enable us to work from your Peace.
To have confidence for the moment, and not hunger restlessly for results.
To set upon each hour its full value as part of the whole education of the child.
And when term ends with frayed nerves, still to be wise in the use of time and temper.

M: Jesus says 'Come, follow Me'

P: Keep us through the Holy Spirit's work, in the thrill and awe of our calling, for the sake of the Kingdom. Amen.

Comments

A very well-planned act of worship for teachers which would be useful for a staff service or for a teachers' association. There is clear understanding of the situation that teachers have to face, and this service suggests the type of worship that could be worked out for other professions. Some of the responses might prove rather long and involved. It is not easy for a group to read long passages together, especially when the matter is unfamiliar.

Further Comment

The responses should be briefer and most of their contents gathered into biddings.

F. ORDER OF SERVICE FOR A HOUSE CHURCH

Source: Rev. Richard Jones

Leader: A prayer asking the Holy Spirit to inspire us
All: The Lord's Prayer

Leader: Late that night when the disciples were together, Jesus came and stood among them. 'Peace be with you' he said, and then showed them his hands and his side. So when the disciples saw the Lord they were filled with joy.
All: May this joy be ours, through Jesus Christ our Lord.

Leader: Let us thank God that this is His world in which He is now at work. What is he doing? Here are the words which Christ used to describe his work:

Reader: The Spirit of the Lord is upon me because he has anointed me; he has sent me to announce good news to the poor, to proclaim release for prisoners and recovery of sight for the blind; to let the broken victims go free; to proclaim the year of the Lord's favour.

Leader: Let us think of the ways in which God is doing these things today, and make them into our thanksgiving
All: (Discuss together how these things can be seen today).

Leader: A prayer of thanksgiving for the work of the living God

Leader: Let us consider together the most urgent causes for which money is needed. All money belongs finally to God. (After determining the cause, an offering for it is taken and someone deputed to see that it reaches the right destination)

Reader: A passage from a modern translation of the Bible

Leader: Let us consider together the most serious sins in the world, those made plain by today's newspaper.
All: (Discuss together these sins)

113

Leader:	A prayer of confession for these sins, especially those in which we play an obvious part, making use of the bidding by the Leader, 'Lord, hear our prayer,' after which ALL join in the response 'And let our cry come unto Thee'
Leader:	A brief explanation of a Christian truth.
Leader:	Jesus said 'Are not five sparrows sold for twopence and yet not one of them is overlooked by God? Moreover the hairs of your head are all numbered'. Let us think of our special needs and those of people living round here or known to us
All:	(Mention these needs)
Leader:	Prayers for these needs, using the bidding and response as before
All:	May the grace of the Lord Jesus Christ, and the love of God, and the fellowship of the Holy Spirit, be with us all evermore. Amen.

Comments

1. This is an order which takes into account the advantages and needs of a situation where a small group meets in informal circumstances. There is adequate opportunity for personal contributions to the service, while preserving an ordered framework that prevents the service becoming trivial and chatty. There is real sharing here, all of which would help to bring the group into fellowship with each other.

2. Such a service could not be used too often. This is to be expected, since informality does not thrive on repetition.

G. A GUEST SERVICE

Source: Rev. A. G. K. Esdaile, St. Mary's, Wimbledon

Please make yourselves feel at home as far as you can when you arrive in church. Introduce yourself to your neighbour or have a few words with a friend, if you wish.

At 6.30 there will be a practice of the music we shall be singing. This will be followed by silent preparation for our worship, our listening, and our prayer. We know that God is among us if we are meeting in his name.

Opening Hymn 159:	'Now thank we all our God'
Responses:	(Part of Psalm 47 translated by Joseph Gelineau)

114

Priest loudly:	All peoples, clap your hands,
People loudly:	Cry to God with shouts of joy.
Priest:	Sing praise to God, sing praise
People:	Sing praise to our king, sing praise
Priest:	God is king of all the earth. Sing praise with all your skill
People:	The rulers of the earth belong to God. To God who reigns over all.
Modern Psalm:	The Lord of the Dance (Music traditional. Words: Sydney Carter)
1st Reading:	Acts 17: 16-34. St. Paul is irritated by the idols that he finds on his visit to Athens. He makes a speech to the 'gentlemen' of Athens, in which he stresses the unity of God and the resurrection of Christ.

The readings will be followed by a few moments' silence

2nd Reading:	Michel Quoist—'I would like to rise very high.' If only we knew how to look at life as God sees it, we should realize that nothing is secular in the world, but that everything contributes to the building of the kingdom of God. To have faith is not only to raise one's eyes to God to contemplate him; it is also to look at the world—but with Christ's eyes.
Creed:	Hymn 65: 'Firmly I believe and truly'
Kneel for prayer	O God we don't find it easy to believe in you; (said together): We know we are often too selfish and busy; Forgive us for not bothering about you, about people; About our neighbours and their needs more than our own. We haven't thought about really loving as you love— What it means, what it costs. Wrench us out of these ruts, even if it hurts, Into caring as Jesus did. Amen.

115

Priest:	O God you see us gathered here to worship you in our singing, our prayer, and our listening. Help us to remember that we know more about you because Jesus, your son, was born in poverty nearly two thousand years ago. Help us to remember that Jesus is with us now. We ask you to wipe out what we have done against you, and our friends, and our enemies. Help us to keep firmly to what is right and good, through Jesus Christ our Lord.
All:	Our Father in heaven, your name is honoured and praised. Help us to carry out your wishes upon earth, as they are carried out in heaven. Please supply us with our day to day needs and forgive us our sins as we try to forgive people who do wrong against us. Do not let us be persuaded to do wrong and deliver us from evil, as all power and glory belongs to you for ever. Amen.
Hymn 68:	'God of mercy, God of Grace'
Address and discussion:	'What on earth *is* the Church?'
Closing prayers	led by a member of the congregation If anyone wishes to add their own intercessions, there will be the opportunity. If you do this it would help if you would be quite brief and follow this pattern: 'Let us pray for . . .' (pause) 'Lord in your mercy,'
Answer:	'Hear our prayer'.
Final Hymn 236:	'The Church's one foundation'
All kneel	
Responses:	
Priest loudly:	You are no longer aliens in a foreign land
People loudly:	But fellow-citizens with God's people, Members of God's household.
Priest:	You are built upon the foundation laid by the apostles and prophets.

People:	And Christ Jesus himself is the foundation-stone.
Priest:	In him the whole building is bonded together
People:	In him we are being built into a spiritual dwelling for God.

The Blessing

Note:

The hymns referred to here are from *Hymns Ancient and Modern*. The reading of Michel Quoist's Prayer is from p.11 of *Prayers of Life*.

Comments

1. This service was planned for a rather lush suburban church, and therefore for the type of congregation that will be at home with Quoist, Carter, and Gelineau. All the best materials are used.

2. It is interesting to hear the Anglicans encouraging chatter (neighbourly) before the service. Perhaps we in Methodism have not been so wrong? The practice for the service both breaks the ice and allows for all sorts of explanation and preparation. This also brings the situation under control and after a silence the service can proceed.

3. The opening is joyful and welcoming, but did the people clap their hands? A pity if they didn't. The great traditional hymn is eminently suitable for a guest service, especially if the traditional tune was used. Too much innovation might confuse, and spoil the freshness of the Sydney Carter. Does the singing of the Creed ask too much of a guest congregation? Not all would be able to subscribe to such a full statement of faith. Similarly the ending of the service presumes rather a lot. It suggests that the congregation are already fully integrated into the household of God, whereas in fact many would be still enquirers. These should be assured that God goes with them, muddled as they may be, into a world where they will meet muddle and doubt.

4. The confession following the lessons and Creed contains a right mixture of faith and doubt, though the assurance of the Priest is rather involved and distracting. The version of the Lord's Prayer is helpful.

5. Altogether it is a lively and interesting experiment and in fact was the first of several such services which all have the same vigour.

H. HARVEST FESTIVAL

Source: Rev. Peter Webb, Biggin Hill Baptist Church

Call to Worship

Hymn 962:   'Come ye thankful people, come'

Prayers of Adoration and Confession

The Lord's Prayer

Hymn 851:   'All things bright and beautiful'
>   During this hymn the Minister will receive the harvest gifts
>   from the Junior Church.

First Lesson: Deuteronomy 8: 6-18
                 Psalm 65 (No. 38 in hymn book)

Second Lesson: II Corinthians 9: 1-15

The stewards will wait on the congregation for the gifts of money
Presentation of Gifts from the Family of the Church
>   Let us with a gladsome mind
>   Praise the Lord, for He is kind:
>   For His mercies aye endure,
>   Ever faithful, ever sure.

The verses that follow are to be sung during the presentation of the
different gifts

THE GIFT OF BREAD
Presented by two fathers

Minister: The eyes of all wait upon Thee, O Lord
Congregation: And Thou givest them their meat in due season

Fathers: We, bread-winners of this community, present to
                 God, bread, the staff of life, as a token of our
                 gratitude for his sending all things that are needful
                 both for our souls and bodies.

Minister: Let us pray for all those whose daily work provides
                 our food and clothing; those who work on land and
                 sea; and let us remember that man does not live by
                 bread alone.
>   Praise Him for our harvest store.
>   He hath filled the garner floor.
>   For His mercies aye endure,
>   Ever faithful, ever sure.

118

THE GIFT OF MILK
Presented by two mothers

Minister: Thou openest Thine hand

Congregation: And fillest all things with plenteousness

Mothers: We mothers of this community present to God, milk, as a token of our gratitude for His loving care and as a symbol of human kindness for His children and the sick.

Minister: Let us pray for all the homes and hospitals in our land and for our church as it ministers the milk of the word, that we may grow unto salvation.

    All things living He doth feed,
    His full hand supplies their need;
    For His mercies aye endure,
    Ever faithful, ever sure.

THE GIFT OF FRUIT AND VEGETABLES
Presented by three young people

Minister: He brought forth grass for the cattle

Congregation: And green herb for the service of men.

Your Person: We, the youth of this community, present to God our gift of the fruits of the earth as a token of our gratitude and as a symbol of the high trust committed to us.

Minister: Let us pray for schools, youth organizations, training colleges and universities, that young people may grow in the knowledge of our Saviour, to follow Christ the King and enthrone Him in their hearts for ever.

    And hath bid the fruitful field
    Crops of precious increase yield,
    For His mercies aye endure,
    Ever faithful, ever sure.

THE GIFT OF FLOWERS
Presented by four children

Minister: Consider the lilies of the field how they grow

Congregation: Even Solomon in all his glory was not arrayed like one of these.

Child: We, the children of this community, present these flowers, to say 'thank you' for all the beautiful things in God's world.

119

| Minister: | Let us pray that the beauties of the earth may teach us the beauty of God's love and goodness, and that we may enable our children to grow up in love and understanding. |

<blockquote>
Praise Him that He made the sun
Day by day its course to run:
For His mercies aye endure,
Ever faithful, ever sure.
</blockquote>

THE GIFTS OF INDUSTRY
Presented by three industrial workers

| Minister: | Whatsoever thy hand findeth to do |
| Congregation: | Do with all thy might. |

| Worker: | We workers from industry representing all in this community who follow any trade, craft, or calling, present these gifts to God as a token of our gratitude for his wondrous gifts to men. |

| Minister: | Let us pray that in industry and in commerce there may be freedom from distrust, bitterness, and dispute. May we all seek what is just and equal, and may we all live together in unity and love. |

<blockquote>
He with all-commanding might
Filled the new-made world with light:
For His mercies aye endure,
Ever faithful, ever sure
</blockquote>

THE GIFT OF MONEY
Presented by two stewards

| Minister: | Bear one another's burdens |
| Congregation: | And so fulfil the law of Christ. |

| Steward: | We, the stewards of this church, present the offering of this congregation, a token gift of all our possessions which are a trust from God. |

| Minister: | Let us pray that Christians everywhere may be known for their industry, their right use of leisure, their sacrificial giving, and their honest, kindly dealing with one another, as those striving to love God and their neighbour as themselves. |

<blockquote>
Let us blaze His name abroad;
For of gods He is the God:
For His mercies aye endure,
Ever faithful, ever sure.
</blockquote>

120

THE GIFT OF BREAD AND WINE
Presented by two deacons

Minister: As often as you eat this bread, and drink this cup
Congregation: You proclaim the Lord's death until He come.

Deacon: We present this bread and this wine, that by partici-
pating in the sacrament we may feed on Christ by
faith.

Minister: Let us pray that as the wheat scattered over the
field has been harvested into this one loaf, so the
Church may be gathered together from the ends of
the earth into Christ's kingdom, and that offering
ourselves as a living sacrifice we may be strengthened
to go forth into the world to serve God faithfully.

And for richer food than this,
Pledge of everlasting bliss:
For His mercies aye endure;
Ever faithful, ever sure.
Glory to our bounteous King:
Glory let creation sing.
For His mercies aye endure
Ever faithful, ever sure.

Prayers of Thanksgiving, Intercession and Petition

Hymn 963: 'We plough the fields and scatter'
Blessing
(sung Amen)

Comments

1. This is a family service with plenty of action, using a large
number of people. There is constant movement that should help
such a service to come alive and to interest all ages. There is nothing
that would test the endurance of those who find it unnatural and
frustrating to be quiet and still. It is simple and direct, making excellent use of a great traditional harvest hymn to bring together the
various elements of offering.

2. Although the language is stilted in places, it is generally simple
and dignified. There is a deliberate attempt to link together the life
of the world and that of the church. It is possibly a little sentimental
over flowers as the tokens of providence. Why in the offering were
there not actual minerals and products of industry? Harvests are
not only vegetable.

3. The link of the bread of the fields with the bread of the Eucharist is excellent, but why was not the Communion celebrated?
Should we at any time display the bread and the wine without
celebrating?

Further Comments

1. This is one of the few services in the book which has a prayer of thanksgiving as its climax, a feature which is greatly to be desired.

2. Would it be possible to heighten the exultation by putting in some dancing by the children?

3. A service like this is bound to raise the question of its relation to the Eucharist. This is done pointedly here by using the eucharistic prayer from the Didache.

I.   BREAD IS MADE FOR LAUGHTER

Source: Brian Frost (via Christian Aid)

This is one of a series of services that might be called 'propaganda acts' which were originally published by Christian Aid and are now obtainable through: Galliard Ltd., Queen Anne Road, Great Yarmouth, Norfolk.

Other services include: *No Man is an Island* (an excellent anthology on the world need); *Standing in the Rain; I am the World's Surplus Man; Put Your Hand in Mine and Walk on; Different From Us.*

The present service is designed to awaken the conscience of the Church to world need at a time when it is celebrating the abundance of harvest. The situation is presented factually and interpreted in the light of Christian worship, that of thanksgiving and the communion. It is scripted for three readers and a commentator, making use of both traditional harvest hymns (sometimes ironically) and folk songs on the theme of world need. The script is racy and pungent, but too long to be printed in full. An outline gives the gist of the service:

The READERS declare the goodness of God.

The CONGREGATION respond with three verses of the familiar hymn:
> 'Yes, God is Good' (968)

God is good, but India and China starve.

It is easy to celebrate harvest in the affluent West but, for most, life is bread with bitterness.

Yet we want to celebrate harvest—so the congregation sings:
> 'Come, ye thankful people, come' (962)

Three people speak from their experience:
> A Vietnamese,
> A go-ahead girl from the West,
> A reporter who has seen it all—affluence and poverty.

Folk Song: 'It's a funny old world'

But it is not just a matter of personal charity

Folk Song: 'The rich man's crumbs'

The Bible reminds us of a new order where compassion will be expressed socially:

The CONGREGATION reads: Isaiah 35 responsively.
Disease and hunger must be overcome, not just met.

Folk song: 'Hungry now'

This is a problem of community. The Gospel talks of community. The bread we eat speaks of community. Bread that Jesus took and broke. Bread that he gave to a divided community.

So we meet in communion as a community and cannot sincerely take part without our neighbour. No neighbour—no communion.

Folk song: 'Dives and Lazarus'

Community responsibility means politics. Christian love is both personal and political.

A speaker elaborates on the politics of development and its meaning for us at Harvest. A short talk lasting about eight minutes.

The COMMENTATOR continues:

Politics alone is not enough. The grim political systems that forget the personal show this. 'The job of the Christian is with both political and personal bread . . . for the only real way of having bread is having it with laughter. The only way of having it with laughter is to rule with God over the world with the king of laughter . . . for twenty years or so a worker at a bench.'

Hymn 963: 'We plough the fields and scatter'

PRAYER: Hunger: Michel Quoist.

Prayers of Intercession with the response:
Reader: Help us, O Lord, to make known your rule
People: And assert that Christ is King.

The OFFERING: made with this communal offering by the congregation:

We offer to you, Lord, our money. We offer to you, Lord, ourselves. We offer to you the work of the world in this neighbourhood and beyond.

Grant that men may work with joy and dignity.

Grant that men may have bread with laughter.

And grant that we may reflect in our work and in our lives
The community we have found in the sharing of the loaf
And the risen presence we have known in the breaking of the bread.
Amen.

Folk songs: 'Judas and Mary'

123

Notes:

1. The following folk songs came from *Songs from Notting Hill* (obtainable from Lancaster Road Methodist Church, London W11, price one shilling):

'It's a funny Old World'

'Hungry Now'

'Dives and Lazarus'

2. 'The rich man's crumbs' is from 'Songs from the Square' (obtainable from Christian Aid, 10 Eaton Gate, London, SW1, price two shillings and sixpence).

3. 'Judas and Mary' is from *Nine Carols or Ballads* by Sydney Carter (from the Christian Aid Shop, 167 Sloane Street, London, SW6, price five shillings).

Comments:

1. As a propaganda act the aim of this service is to get over a message rather than to present a complete act of worship. But this service shows how forms of worship can be used to emphasize a theme. Hymns of thanksgiving, scripture reading, the Communion, and prayer provoke by their very nature reflexion upon the theme of Bread with Laughter. They are used both to stress false attitudes of worship and to suggest positive lines of action. In fact the service is something of a commentary on the meaning of worship, its dangers and its necessity.

2. The ordering of the elements of worship is interesting:

Affirmation of the Goodness of God (in a hungry world!)

Consternation—rather than confession

The Ministry of the Word—pointing to hope and responsibility

This expounded in terms of the Communion

Confession in the Prayer: Hunger

Intercessions

The Offering

This shows that the pattern of worship need not be neglected when there is an urgent message to convey. In fact the elements of worship endorse and emphasize the theme.

Further Comments

1. This has all the elements of worship plus a touch of genius.

2. Should hymns be used ironically, as the introduction suggests? Possibly this use here could be defended by saying that they contrast in a creative way with other aspects of truth expounded in the service.

124

J. A VISION OF JUDGEMENT (Part I)

Source: Dr. Erik Routley

This is the first of a series of four services based on the Book of Revelation. It shows how Bible instruction can be presented in a service in a dramatic and vivid manner. It also suggests an alternative to the normal Sunday evening service when there is a small number of people who will have already worshipped that day. Dr. Routley describes his intention and method:

'The idea was to get out something which could be put on with the minimum of rehearsal. I turned the choir into a troupe of players, and all the rehearsal we got was the 45 minutes which we normally devote to choir practice before the evening service. So of course the whole thing was read. This didn't matter: it gave us the chance to get more said. We used the choir rostrum, the pulpit, various parts of the gallery, and at once point a position behind the congregation.'

Since the service is very full, it is only possible to give an outline of it; but this will indicate how the material was presented.

THE PROLOGUE (from the Rostrum):

A Commentator sets the scene by describing Asia Minor, the land of the seven churches of the Apocalypse. He uses a map and adds modern references. He mentions and reads from the letters that Paul wrote to Colossae and Ephesus, and this introduces the letters of John Presbyter.

As the Congregation sing the hymn 'Holy, Holy, Holy,' John goes to the pulpit.

Voices from the Gallery:

1. Holy, Holy, Holy is God the Sovereign Lord of all, who was and is and is to come.

2. Thou art worthy, O Lord our God, to receive Glory and Honour and Power, because thou didst create all things; by thy will they were created and have their being.

3. Worthy is the Lamb that was slain, to receive all power and wealth, wisdom and might, honour, glory, and praise!

4. Praise and Honour, Glory and might, to him who sits on the throne and to the Lamb for ever!

John then reads the account of his call from Revelation 1.

The Commentator: Interprets the passage and then pictures the seven churches, describing the situation of the Early Church in terms of present-day places and situations. The worship of the Church is described and the Eucharist acted out by the

Choir with someone taking the part of the Bishop. The service is broken up by a police raid and a court scene is described. The choir returns and the hymn, 'O Gladsome light' is sung.

After this the three Roman Emperors of the time, Nero, Vespasian, and Domitian introduce themselves, describing their attitudes to the Christians (biographical research will have to be done here). Domitian ends his diatribe against Christians and their like by saying:

Anybody who doesn't call me God gets hell.

In response the congregation breaks in with the hymn,
'Rejoice, the Lord is King ...
The keys of death and hell are to our Jesus given'

John then appears and reads the seven letters, with members of the choir making gazetteer comments as each of the places is mentioned, e.g.:

JOHN: The seven candlesticks are the seven churches. So I wrote this to the church at Ephesus.

Gaz. 1: Ephesus: The largest seaport in Asia Minor, the old capital of Ionia. Parts of the city were already standing in the sixth century BC. *See* the temple of Diana, rebuilt 356 BC, part of which is now the temple of the goddess Roma and the divine leader Julius.

John: You have put to the proof those who claim to be apostles, etc.

John then leaves the pulpit and, taking a chair at the front, he is interviewed by a Twentieth Century Man, as if this were a television programme.

In this way the letters are explained and discussed, with details being clarified. The passionate visionary is clearly contrasted to the moderate man of today and the interview ends briskly:

Interviewer: You're not particularly optimistic, then?

John: No, I am not an optimist. I am a believer.

Interviewer: John Presbyter, thank you very much.

The Bishop then closes with a prayer of praise and intercession, followed by the Lord's Prayer.

The Peace is given and the congregation disperse after singing:
'The head that once was crowned with thorns'

126

Comments

1. This was felt to be an excellent presentation of a Biblical theme. The synopsis does little justice to the vigour of the script which makes full use of the Scottish situation in which the service was held. This synopsis will, however, indicate the great variety of ways in which information can be presented dramatically without the service becoming a lecture. Since the service is read it would not be difficult to produce, but it would demand experienced readers.

2. The hymns provide an opportunity for congregational response and involvement, but apart from these there is no place where the congregation actively takes part. This is partly due, we understand, to the Scottish situation which does encourage spoken responses, but also to the fact that the service is conceived in terms of a drama in which spoken responses would be misplaced. This is an issue which has to be judged in the light of the local situation and there will be places where the atmosphere built up by a dramatic sequence would be broken by a formal response. The unspoken response can often be deeper. On the other hand, where we have a dramatic service it may be valuable to provide some kind of response other than a hymn for the whole congregation. This demands, however, that the congregation be thought of a taking part during the whole service, and its being used as the choir is used here. Also the congregation would need to be rehearsed as the choir was. This is not easy but could add greatly to the value of a service.

6. Youth Services

THIS IS THE sphere in which experimentation is often attempted and most readily accepted. It is also the sphere where there are most hazards. To insert a Beaumont tune (already hackneyed), a folk song, or a pop group item into an otherwise conventional service does no justice to worship or to youth.

Young people are usually more ready than others to prepare worship as a team. This provides an opportunity for thinking through ideas and discussing the structure and purpose of worship. Suitability and relevance to the theme should guide the planning rather than novelty, but the possibilities of the building, the congregation, and the resources of the team should be exploited to the full. Time should be given for individual preparation and research, and rehearsal should be thorough.

The danger will be to let interesting items determine the nature of the service, and this can lead to a shapeless string of features that have little purpose or cohesion. It is important, therefore, to think out the aim and purpose of a service before coming to decide on individual items. In team preparation it is very easy to forget the congregation, and so every effort should be made to incorporate them into the service. Where necessary the whole congregation should share in rehearsal for the act of worship. This can in itself be made a valuable part of worship.

Further introductory comment

The total impression of the following services is that they tend to be more aware of the world than of the gospel—or rather, they lack a dominating sense of the offer of God in Christ (what used to be called the objectivity of Grace). They are in danger of Pelagianism (making religion into a matter of what men can achieve) and while they should help to awaken slumbering consciences they may not adequately sustain Christian lives. They try to begin where people are, which is laudable, but some of them are not sufficiently conscious of the given-ness of the gospel. At this point it is easy to distinguish those services which have had the guidance of a competent theologian from those which are more amateurish.

Whilst much of the material is didactic, this is all right if moralizing and priggishness are avoided. On the whole these services are satisfactory in this respect.

A. A FOLK SERVICE:
'LIVING TOGETHER'

Source: Revs. Tom Duerden and B. D. Brown

Introduction by Commentator: 'The Lordship of Christ' (A Prayer from a Bristol Youth Club)

> Christ is the Lord of the smallest atom,
> Christ is the Lord of outer space,
> Christ is the Lord of the constellations,
> Christ is the Lord of every place;
>> Of the furthest star,
>> Of the coffee bar,
>> Of the length of the Berlin Wall;
>> Of the village green,
>> Of the Asian scene,
>> Christ is the Lord of All.
>
> Christ is the Lord of the human heart-beat,
> Christ is the Lord of every breath,
> Christ is the Lord of a Man's existence,
> Christ is the Lord of life and death.
> Christ is the Lord of our thoughts and feelings,
> Christ is the Lord of all we plan,
> Christ is the Lord of man's decision,
> Christ is the Lord of total man.
>> In the local street where the people meet,
>> In the church or the nearby hall,
>> In the factory,
>> In the family,
>> Christ is the Lord of all.
>
> Christ is the Lord of our love and courtship,
> Christ is the Lord of man and wife,
> Christ is the Lord of the things we care for,
> Christ is the Lord of all our life.

Commentator: Let us look through the eyes of the Press at 'The World in action' and see its needs and problems by contrasting excerpts taken from newspapers in recent months. As we hear these words let us remember those in need and help them.

The World's Press reports:

Reader 1: 'Indian Parliament'. The marchers shouted protests about the food shortages; banners included —'India must have the atom bomb.'

Commentator:	These are the facts, however:
Reader 2:	The diet of an Indian is 1,700 calories; they need 2,500 calories. 92% have eye trouble.
Commentator:	The Press again:
Reader 3:	India prepares to join Nuclear Club.
Reader 1:	Pakistan has been spending 48% of her total revenue on defence services. India has been spending one-third of her revenue on defence.
Reader 2:	Half the babies born in India reach adult age. India and Pakistan are poor.
Commentator:	But these are the facts:
Reader 4:	Never before in the history of the world was there so much wealth; never before was there so much poverty. Never before was there so much food; never before was there so much hunger.
Commentator:	Just listen to this from the Wealthy West:
Reader 1:	Americans smoked 533,000 million cigarettes in the year ending yesterday.
Reader 2:	In 1964 Britain spent nearly £7,000 million on food and drink and £2,400 million on entertainments.
Folk Group:	'Does nobody care?'
Commentator:	But in another newspaper tucked away we found:
Reader 3:	Old age pensioner dies of malnutrition and neglect.
Reader 2:	Thalidomide Babies' need of world aid.
Reading:	'Indifference'—Mime.
Commentator:	It is all very mysterious, as Bob Dylan shows:
All sing:	'Blowin' in the Wind'
Commentator:	Flashback—
Reader 4:	From a correspondent—A young man asked: 'What shall I do that I may live?' Jesus said 'Go and give to the poor.' He went away sad, because he was wealthy.

130

Reader 3:	'For the message you have heard from the beginning is this: that we should love one another.'
Reader 4:	1 John 3: 13-17 (N.E.B.)
Solo:	'Lonely Road'
Reader 1:	From a foreign correspondent: 'They passed by . . . but he came where he was and took care of him. Then said Jesus: "Go, and do likewise." ' Pause for thought:
Commentator:	Let us pray together— O God, you taught us through Jesus Christ in the parable of the Good Samaritan that charity begins away from home, that the superfluities of the rich are the necessities of the poor, that the earth was made for all men and not for the advantage of the few; help us to sort out our values.
All sing:	'Kumbaya Lord'
Reader 5:	Never before in the history of the world was there so much wealth: Never before was there so much poverty: Never before was there so much education: never before so little knowledge: Never before so much power, never before was that power so prepared to be used for the destruction of human life.
Reader 1:	What can we do about this: In our small, narrow lives we can do nothing to ease international tension, to change the mutual suspicions of East and West.
Reader 2:	But we can get at the human root of this disease of mistrust—we can change our minds about those we dislike.
Congregation:	Lord, use the gifts you have given us to ease our neighbour's needs.
Reader 3:	We can take an interest, a real and active interest, in those we find tedious or do not understand.

Congregation:	Lord, use the gifts you have given us to ease our neighbour's needs.
Reader 4:	Worries can be shared if we have the patience to listen.
Congregation:	Lord, use the gifts you have given us to ease our neighbour's needs.
Reader 5:	Nothing is too small. To carry a suitcase for a weary stranger might require courage as well as physical strength.
Congregation:	Lord, use the gifts you have given us to ease our neighbour's needs.
Commentator:	But there is good news to be found in the Press. Young people do respond to need. Listen to this.
Reader 1:	Ten young men, average age twenty-two, fly out to the West Indies. They are giving up their jobs and their pay packets for eight weeks to build a dairy plant on the poverty-stricken island of St. Vincent.
Reader 2:	Students walked from Edinburgh to Land's End via London. They raised nearly £3 a mile for Save the Children Fund—a total of £2,300.
Reader 3:	Young people in Seaton Delaval distribute 4,200 Christmas Family Boxes for Oxfam to help the world's needy.
Reader 4:	Youth join forces to help aged. Salford's 130 Youth Organizations are to form a reservoir of volunteer labour to help the City's old people. They hope to distribute Christmas food parcels to at least 4,000.
Reader 5:	600 young people from Churches and Youth Clubs in the Newcastle area hike from Newcastle to Carter Bar, raising £2,300 for the Richard Dimbleby Cancer Research Fund. 100 young people from the Northumberland Association of Youth Clubs beat the boundaries of the City of Newcastle to raise funds for the Spastics Society.
Commentator:	Young people of the Methodist Association of Youth Clubs, raise over £90,000 to build a hospital in Dabou in the Ivory Coast.

132

All:	The Lord's Prayer.
All sing:	'When I needed a neighbour, were you there?' (Offertory taken during singing)
Commentator: All say together:	May the strength of God pilot us, May the power of God preserve us, May the wisdom of God instruct us, May the hand of God protect us, May the way of God direct us, May the shield of God defend us, May the host of God guard us against the snares of evil and the temptations of the world; May Christ be with us, Christ before us, Christ in us, Christ over us; May Thy salvation, O Lord, be always ours This day, and forever more. Amen.

Notes

The poem 'Indifference' is from *Rhymes*, by Studdert-Kennedy.

The folk songs are most easily obtained from *60 Folk Songs* edited by Peter Smith, published by Galliard.

Comments

1. Folk music with its social concern and its questioning about the issues of life lends itself well to what might be called secular worship, especially when it is used with statistics and comments about the society we live in. Both these feature in this service and the material used here is suitable and effective. Statements about world need are followed by comment and then by Biblical references (though some of these are not very relevant).

2. But neither is the theme developed, nor is the structure of the worship evident. The opening, for instance, is indecisive. The affirmation of the Lordship of Christ should lead to some response to the fact that Christ is Lord, but the focus is directed to the problems of the world. However, before we get to these, we sing 'We shall overcome' (a hymn more suitable for the end of a service than the beginning) and only then we are faced with the stark facts of poverty and affluence which are the real issue of the service. If only the service had begun with these statistics, the whole aim of the service would have become clear from the start. It is as if the people

preparing the service had a lot of good material and they did not want to leave anything out. This weakness of structure is evident throughout.

3. Opportunities to bring in the congregation are missed, especially where prayer is concerned. The statements made cry out for responses, for confessions, for intercessions and petitions. Worship becomes effective where this response is given adequate expression in prayer or hymn singing. It is essential that at each stage of the service we should ask what response we expect from the congregation and how we are to help them to make it.

Further Comments

This is a demonstration, rather than an act of worship (hence he absence of liturgical shape). The tendency to display the achievement of young Christians in contrast to the selfishness of the world is unevangelical, to say the least.

B. THE TWO CITIES

Source: Rev. David Head

SILENCE

AFFIRMATION (standing)

V: We have seen a city
R: A city like all other cities

V: We have glimpsed the city of God
R: Judging and penetrating this city and all cities

V: The word of God
R: To us and all in the city

V: Except the Lord build the house
R: They labour in vain that build it

V: Except the Lord keep the city
R: The watchman wakes but in vain.

HYMN OF PRAISE 4:
        'From all that dwell below the skies'

CONFESSION (seated)

V: When the stranger says: 'What is the meaning of this city?
        Do you huddle close together because you love each other?'
        what will you answer?

R1:	(all downstairs) We all dwell together to make money from each other
R2:	(all upstairs) This is a community
R1:	We have to live
R2:	We have yet to learn to live
R1:	No man knows or cares who is his neighbour
R2:	He who loves God must also love his brother
R1:	How rich I am, and how well I have done; I have everything I want in the world
R2:	What shall it profit a man if he gain the whole world, and lose his own soul?
R1:	Egypt and Greece, goodbye, and goodbye Rome
R2:	The city of God remaineth.

LEADER

Today we have seen the city, and the choice. We confess with all mankind our tendency to use and abuse each other, and to make ourselves gods or slaves.

V:	If we have superficially spoken of 'God over all and in all'
R:	Forgive us and simplify our faith.
V:	If we have heard Christ's call to freedom through responsibility, maturity through self-giving, and have been afraid
R:	Forgive us and show us our high calling
V:	If we have become idealists or cynics, and have forgotten the Holy Spirit who lifts up our hearts and keeps us down to earth,
R:	Forgive us and make us whole.

LEADER

God the Father who has prepared for us a city,
God the Son who sees the city and weeps over it,
God the Holy Spirit who judges our disharmony and brings community,
May the one God, incomprehensible, forgive us and enable us to forgive one another; give us our status as citizens and make us free for others; reveal his disturbing presence and the secret of personal victory.

R:	He who is victorious—I will write the name of my God upon him, and the name of the city of my God, and my own new name.

ANTHEM   (Psalm 48)

1.

Great is the Lord
And greatly to be praised,
In the city of our God.
Beautiful the site,
Wonderfully raised,
Is the city (3 times) of the great
   King.

2. (Congregation)

The city of God is His holy Church,
The people of God who can never fall.
The city is built on the rock of faith,
And God is the builder and refuge of all.
The city stands high as Jerusalem did,
Set on a hill, and it cannot be hid.

3.

We have seen with our eyes,
We have heard with our ears,
The deeds of our Saviour King:
Doubt and anger and greed took
   flight,
Broken and sunk are the ships of
   night.
We have heard,
We have seen:
Our loving witness we bring.

4. (Congregation)

So now of a city on earth we sing,
The place of our home and our up-
   bringing,
Where cranes pierce the sky and the sky
   lines change
And shops and factories are concrete and
   strange
Draw the inner and outer ring,
Making a crown for Christ the King.

5.

Here in this our city
Dwell Thy people, O Lord;
Here in this Thy temple
Thou art greatly adored.
Our thoughts are of thy loving
   kindness.
We celebrate Thy tender mercy.
As Thy name
Is Thy praise and worth,
Here and the same
To the ends of the earth.

6. (Congregation)

Thy will for the city is peace and truth
Establish our hearts in the days of youth.
We live in the gladness of Christ who
   died,
The Lord who is risen will be our Guide.
Under Thy hand is our lives' endeavour;
God is our God for ever and ever.

7. (Congregation)

Repeat 1.

Words: David Head (C.20)
Music: Stanley Mountford

LESSONS (seated)

LEADER: We read of two cities; first, the city of Rome (called
Babylon), corrupt at heart, bringing judgement upon
itself;
then of a city with firm foundation, whose architect
and builder is God.

READER 1:   Revelation 18: 1, 2, 5, 9-20 (NEB)

READER 2:   Revelation 21: 5-7, 10, 22-27

HYMN 703:   'City of God how broad and far'

ADDRESS

HYMN 895:   'Where cross the crowded ways of life'

INTERCESSIONS (seated)

Five sets of biddings are given by Group Leaders, beginning 'Let us pray for . . .' and representing the following subjects:
1. Commerce, industry, and advertising
2. Leisure, mass media, and the Church's communication
3. Healthy society and whole persons
4. City redevelopment, housing needs, multi-racial challenge, task of Church
5. The meaning of city life

After each set of biddings:

V: We belong to the city,
R.   We belong to the city of God.
V: O Lord, renew our city,
R: O Lord, renew our lives.

HYMN OF DEDICATION 890

1 Lift up your heads, ye mighty gates
Behold the King of glory waits!
The King of kings is drawing near,
The Saviour of the world is here;
Life and salvation doth He bring,
Wherefore rejoice and gladly sing,
We praise Thee, Father, now,
Creator, wise art Thou!

2 The Lord is just, a helper tried,
Mercy is ever at His side;
His kingly crown is holiness;
His sceptre, pity in distress;
The end of all our woe He brings,
Wherefore the earth is glad and sings.
We praise Thee, Saviour now,
Mighty in deed art Thou!

3 O blest the land, the city blest,
Where Christ the ruler is confest!
O happy hearts and happy homes,
To whom this King in triumph comes!
The cloudless Sun of joy He is.
Who bringeth pure delight and bliss.
O Comforter Divine,
What boundless grace is Thine!

4 Fling wide the portals of your heart,
  Make it a temple set apart
  From earthly use, for heaven's employ,
  Adorned with prayer, and love and joy;
  So shall your Sovereign enter in,
  And new and nobler life begin.
  To Thee, O God, be praise,
  For word and deed and grace.

5 Redeemer come, we open wide,
  Our heart to Thee; here, Lord, abide!
  Thine inner presence let us feel.
  Thy grace and love in us reveal,
  Thy Holy Spirit guide us on,
  Until the glorious goal is won,
  Eternal praise and fame
  We offer to Thy name.

Words: Georg Weissel (C.17)
Tune: Marazion (M. L. Wolstenholm)

During this hymn representatives of Group Sessions bring their banners and stand before the Communion Table, the words on the banners being visible to the congregation.

PRAYER OF DEDICATION (standing)

V: The word of Christ to the contemporary city: This is my city, microcosm of my world. Cities were built to house the gods. This city houses the aspirations of civilized men, the things they strive for and exalt, all they consider good and wise.

R: We find You in all these.

V: Cities were built for protection and peace. This city is wide open to the attacks of the bitter and deprived, the bored and lustful, to the indulgences and deceits of accepted existence, to the threat of sky-borne destruction.

R: We find You in all these.

V: Where men and women work, and families relax together, and children play and quarrel, and young people make independent judgements, I am

R: We find you there.

V: Everywhere my Word is questioned, and my questions are answered. Everywhere my Law in unbreakable, and my laws are broken.

R: All serve You. You serve all.

V: In this city I have a Body, The Church. Men are to see me in its face, and experience me in its deeds. I have other faces and other deeds. My Body is my fullness. I have chosen and sent it, and called you into it. I build it up. In it my judgement begins.

R: Make us Holy as You are holy.

V: My Body represents to the city the unity of mankind. It represents my love for any who might, for any reason whatever, be regarded as the least important of my brothers. I make it holy.

R: Make us holy as You are holy.

V: I love You as a human being made for the city of God. As I love you, so I love all the city. All are mine. And I am for all, and at the side of all. My place is in the holy of holies, and the ungodly of ungodlies. You can come.

R: We would be with You.

V: I have no resting place, no weekend cottage. You have no place to lay your head—except my side. Take the lowest place: that is where you belong. You will find me there.

R: We find You there.

BLESSING

The Lord bless you in the city and country,
                    in home and street,
                    in church and cinema,
                    in suburb and downtown,
                    in school and leisure,
                    in conversation and prayer.

The Lord bless your going out and coming in, now and for evermore.

R: Amen.

Comments

1. An excellent service with a clear and relevant theme that is at the same time thoroughly Biblical, expressed in a telling manner and makes full use of the congregation. It was planned for a schools' festival where hundreds of scholars met together for the first time. Time was taken for rehearsal so that everyone was fully prepared for the worship. The congregation was divided so that the contrasting elements of the theme became apparent.

2. The sacred and the secular are woven throughout the service and the main elements of worship are introduced without losing the centrality of the theme, though certain elements in the hymns do conflict with the thought-forms being used here.

3. The only weakness is the final prayer of dedication. It is a brilliant piece of compressed thought, so much so that the congregation must be left gasping and lost long before the end. Here, more than anywhere else, should the thought and wording be simple and direct so that the worshippers are in no doubt as to the intention of the service.

C. COUNTRY CHURCH YOUTH SERVICE

Source: Wolverton Common Methodist Church

HYMN 452:   'What shall I do my God to love?'

PRAYER:

THE COMMANDMENTS OF THE LORD JESUS

FIRST SPEAKER: Our Circuit as it was

READING: About William Booth and his way of evangelism from *General next to God* by Richard Collier.

SECOND SPEAKER: Our Circuit as it is now

READING: From the *Methodist Recorder* about the problems and opportunities presented by the mobility of the population

HYMN 578:   'A charge to keep I have'

THIRD SPEAKER: Our Circuit as it could be

READING: From the *Methodist Recorder* on the renewal of the Church

HYMN 780:   'Master speak, thy servant heareth'

FOURTH SPEAKER: What can we do about it?

BIBLE READING: John 17: 13-19

SUMMARY: Final Speaker

NOTICES AND OFFERING

HYMN 388:   'My Saviour, how shall I proclaim?'

BENEDICTION

Comments

1. This shows the possibilities of a team service in a small country church where innovation may not be easy and resources few. There is nothing incongruous in the fact that older people share in a youth service. Their experience of the past can be valuable in thinking of the present and future. People who may not wish to preach will be able to speak of their personal experience and this can provide useful material in such a service.

2. The service lacks liturgical structure and has little room for prayer. The development of the theme suggests a pattern of worship and prayer: confession and thanksgiving for the past; intercession for the present, and petition for the future. Such prayer would have involved the congregation, which at present has little to do but listen and sing hymns.

D. FOR THOSE WHO ARE ABOUT TO LEAVE SCHOOL

Source: Rev. Paul Kimber

INTRODUCTION AND WELCOME
(All stand and sing)
       Hymn 28 (5 verses): 'All creatures of our God and King'
(All remain standing)
Reader: We are about to leave school for the wider world;
            Therefore we come together to welcome new freedoms,
                    to give thanks for our heritage,
                    to face the world that waits for us,
                    to set out in the Faith of the Perfect Man.
            And we are met in the presence of God our Father who made us,
               in the comradeship of Christ our Brother who saves us,
               in the power of God the invisible Spirit who inspires us.

WE WELCOME NEW FREEDOMS
(All sit)
Reader: The routines of our former life are passing away now,
            We have outgrown the formal relationships that protected and disciplined us,
            We leave behind the shelter of the secondary school,
            And there will be a decided difference at home.
            The strong regulation of a school's communal life is over,
            And we enter the arena of a free society.

A PRAYER
Reader: Lord, it is Your Will for us to welcome new freedoms,
            We welcome new freedom to embark on a career,
                        freedom to earn our own money, or
                        train to earn it,
                        freedom to spend our money, or save it,
                        freedom to fashion new routines,
                        freedom to plan leisure,
                        freedom to bear new responsibilities,
                        freedom to make fresh meaning out
                        of life.
            We welcome new freedom to grow into the world You
                        have given us,
                        to travel to the destination You have
                        prepared for us,
                        to meet and serve the people You have
                        waiting for us.

Reader: In the challenge of freedom
Leavers: Equip us

Reader: In the decisions of freedom
Leavers: Direct us

Reader: In the art of freedom
Leavers: Discipline us

Reader: In the dangers of freedom
Leavers: Protect us

Reader: In the raptures of freedom
Leavers: Steady us

Reader: In the life of freedom
Leavers: Give us joy

Reader: In the use of freedom
Leavers: Grant us wisdom and the long view

SILENT PRAYER
Reader: In the factory or firm, in college or office,
            In hospital or prison, in city or on the land,
            In coffee bar or on the motorway,
            In whatever place, in whatever condition:

Leavers: We are always free to love our neighbour,
            We are always free to love our God.

SONG: sung by The Citadels

WE GIVE THANKS FOR OUR HERITAGE
Hymn 73 at back of Hymn Book (Ecclesiasticus 44)
Responsive Reading, people and leader saying alternate verses

Reader: Let us now praise those who have given us our immediate
heritage: those from whom we learnt to speak and walk,
to read and write, to think and understand, to know
beauty and to see goodness, to learn of the world and to
recognize God.
There are those who have taught us,
             borne our insults,
             suffered our ignorance.
There are those who have put up with us, and carried us,
             covered up for us, and forgiven us,
             believed in us, and even enjoyed us.
There are those who forced us to work for our own good,
       imposed a sense of order and justice into a muddled
       life, encouraged us when we were despairing.
There are those who laughed with us and not at us,
       who protected us with their understanding when we
       were under fire from others.
There are those whom we have taken for granted.
There are those who have allowed us to take gross
       advantage of them.
And there are those who happen to love us.

SILENT PRAYER

Reader: There need not be jealousy or strife between the
generations.
Let us know comradeship with those who are older,
And comradeship with those who will come after us,
Seeing that we share the same world, and head for the
same destination.

HYMN   10 (2 verses): 'Now thank we all our God'
(Standing)

(All sit)

TO FACE THE WORLD THAT AWAITS US
READING: John 16: 25-33 (NEB)

Reader: We are in the same world, and we shall have trouble;
We are in the same boat, and the boat is being rocked;
We are of the same population, and the population is
exploding;
We are on the same road, and the road is blocked.

143

What a world!

21 million people killed in one war.

Everyone still at a loss to know how to turn enemies into friends and win their way of life without the threat of nuclear disaster.

Two-thirds of the world kept hungry.

130 killed every week on British roads.

Leavers: Now it is our turn to join in;
We shall be responsible too.

A Prayer for Protection

Reader: To bear this responsibility we shall need Your protection, Lord—the armour-plating of Your Spirit! O Lord, protect us!

Reader: Protect us from the big businessmen who see us as industrial fodder
Leavers: Yes Lord, protect us

Reader: From the slick salesmen who treat us as easy market for industrial junk
Leavers: Yes, Lord, protect us

Reader: From the glib advertisements that promise success for the price of a tube of toothpaste
Leavers: Yes, Lord, protect us

Reader: From the pressure of unscrupulous competition, from the status symbol, and the hankering lust for money and position
Leavers: Yes, Lord, protect us

Reader: From those who would foul our minds, soil our bodies, and ignore our spirits
Leavers: Yes, Lord, protect us

Reader: From the world, the bomb, the drug, and the road crash
Leavers: Yes, Lord, protect us

Reader: From ourselves—for we are often our worst enemy
Leavers: Yes Lord, protect us

WE SET OUT IN THE FAITH OF THE PERFECT MAN
Reading: John 8: 31-36 (NEB)

Reader 1: What, free to suffer?
Reader 2: Yes, but to bear it, and make meaning out of it

Reader 1: What, free to stand the relentless din and monotony of the factory?
Reader 2: Yes, but not to be dehumanized by it

Reader 1: What, free to take interminable exams?
Reader 2: Yes, but not to be victimized by them

Reader 1: What, free to be involved in the sins of mankind?
Reader 2: Yes, but to be forgiven by the One upon whom they fall

Reader 1: What, free to believe in a God of love in a world of ruin?
Reader 2: Yes, but not without proving Him true

Reader 1: What, free to die?
Reader 2: Yes, but only to find you are sons and daughters of God, and meant for eternity

Readers 1 Against all the victimization of the world
and 2:   The Son has set us free
           And we are free indeed!
Reader 2: So in the freedom of the Son, the Perfect Man,
                 we shall make money honestly,
                 we shall make love honourably,
                 we shall make time for those who need us,
                 we shall make friends of our enemies,
                 we shall make amends straight away,
                 we shall make Him supreme,
                 for His service in the world is perfect freedom.

Reader 1: The Lord is my Employer
Leavers: I shall never be redundant

Songs   sung by The Citadels

The Address

Hymn   590: 'Forth in thy name, O Lord, I go'
(Standing)

Break for Songs and Refreshments

The Blessing

Note

This service was devised for the St. Albans and District Council of Churches, and was held after the evening services on a July Sunday evening.

Comments

1. This is a service in which the writer has seriously studied the situation and the needs of those who are worshipping. The theme of freedom and responsibility is very much in the thoughts of school leavers. The language is refreshingly informal and yet it does not lack dignity. There is a gentle irony which expresses the dissatisfaction of youth with things as they are and their concern to alter them. Phrases echo formal worship, but the content is contemporary. Full use is made of the litany form so there is abundant response and participation.

2. The reading from Ecclesiasticus sounds somewhat archaic and provides rather an inadequate account of the Christian heritage. This is, however, a favourite passage with Heads and may have been chosen to steady the unconventionality of the rest.

3. The Sermon is badly placed. It should have come much earlier, if at all. But to incorporate songs and refreshments into the service itself is a stroke of genius. It would take, however, a sturdy character (no less than a Brigadier in the original service) to call the company to order for the Blessing.

E. FREEDOM

Source: Rev. James Bates

Congregation: Hymn 36: 'Immortal, invisible, God only wise'

THE FREEDOM OF MAN

God made man to be free

READING	Genesis 1: 1, 26-28
Reader:	From the first moment
	When from the dark confusion
	Of what was not
	There flickered into being
	Light
Man's	There freedom was
freedom is	Growing, widening
seen in his	As worlds wheeled
lordship	As galaxies burst out
over nature	As life in animal and plant
	Developed in complexity
	So freedom grew
	Until in man

146

It reached maturity
Man free to conquer
Free to choose
All things beneath his feet
A master of the elements
At first a beast
Shut in by ignorance and fear
But finding in his hand
And in his brain
A power that subdued and tamed
The wild world to his will
Lord of the beasts
He leaves his mark
In landscape and in cultivated soil
In conurbation and suburban sprawl
In dam and motorway
In seared and blackened acres
And the slum
Where man makes wealth
From earth and human toil
Physicist and Astronaut
Industrialist and Engineer
Artist and Architect
All praise the freedom
God has given to man
But in his Freedom
Does man praise his God?

A PRAYER ON THE M.1

Reader: Lord, it's good to have the foot down on the gas
               The Mini buzzing nicely at a steady 70
               No obstacles or hazards
               The joys of motoring entirely mine
               It's a clean, efficient world
               The Motorway
               With just that touch of smooth frivolity
               (The cups and cutlery in white on blue)
               That makes the Twentieth Century seem to be
               Movement, perpetual motion
               Ever going, and in the going hope.
               Progress, improvement
               There's no end to what with our resources
               We can do
               Just given time.

Lord, give us time
Don't let the motorway end too soon
Don't let us end up in the traffic jam
The meaningless congestion of the city
The place where we arrive
With no purpose but to leave
Give us the pull-in and the roadside bar
The lay-by with a recommended view
The three-star inn, the garage, the Motel
But do not let us stop
For stillness is death
And death breaks the sequence
Stillness makes us think
About our destination
The home that is our home
And not a weekend cottage or a flat
To be escaped to or escape from, week by week.

Reader:	Lord, give us time
People:	Time to be still
Reader:	Time to grow into the world you gave us
People:	Time to grow into the manhood you gave us
All:	And face our destination unafraid

SILENT PRAYER

Reader: Physicist and Astronaut
Industrialist and Engineer
Artist and Architect
All praise the freedom
God has given to man
So in his freedom
Let man praise his God

Congregation: Psalm 150 (Beaumont Setting)
(Seated)

Cantor: Praise the Lord upon the harp
Sing to the harp a song of thanksgiving
Show yourselves joyful before the Lord all ye lands
Sing and rejoice and give thanks
with trumpets also and shawms
O show yourselves joyful before the Lord the King

FREEDOM AND MY NEIGHBOUR

Reader: There is a freedom that man fears
The freedom of his fellow man
In the eye of the tyrant
In the eye of the oppressed

There is no freedom unless man is free in Society	In the eye of the neighbour Who makes his fence too high (or low) In the eye of the traveller in the tube Who, like him, eyes the seat he makes for There is a freedom that threatens That disturbs the freedom he has carved out for himself So we live Shut in by fences, regulations, gates Apartheid in a thousand forms Secures us from the freedom of the world To invade and to destroy Our liberty of isolation For freedom we build our walls For freedom we make our bombs For freedom we pass our laws For freedom we imprison and restrict For freedom we create the Ghetto And we shall meet no one And speak to no one And listen to no one Who does not look as we do Think as we do Act as we do Except at a safe and deferential distance
SONG:	'All Because'

Reader:	Christ came to make men free
	Free from their isolation and their fear
	He came—
	Homeless—and so at home among all
	In poverty—and so the guest of all
	In weakness—and so at the mercy of all
	Common—and so approachable by all
	A man with time for all
	A man for others
	Jesus, Son of Man
	He was in the world
	And nothing came between him and the world
	So that men might be one with him
	And one with each other
	    Mark 2: 15-17a
	    Luke 6: 31-35
	    Luke 14: 12-13

SONG:	'A Cry in the Night' (Geoff Ainger)

Reader: For in our neighbour lies
                      The secret of our happiness
                      He alone can liberate
                      The generous instinct
                      And dispel the fear
                      That shuts us in

Reader: But the man, wanting to justify himself said: But
                      who is my neighbour?

Reader: I looked for my neighbour in the city
                      I looked for the person who had time to be
                      Neighbour to me
                      The churches were open, but no one was there
                      The chapels were securely locked
                      In the offices there was no time to talk
                      In factories the din too great
                      The rushing and the hazards of the street
                      Made conversation dangerous
                      Where people lived no door stood open
                      And no one stood upon the threshold
                      To pass the time of day
                      What threshold has a flat?
                      How can you welcome in the passer-by
                      At fifteen stories up?
                      Where was it that men gathered and men talked
                      Where they had time
                      Time for each other
                      And, perhaps, some time for God?

PRAISE GOD FOR COFFEE BARS
Reader: Let us praise God for Coffee Bars
                      Praise him for
                      The dim and unreligious light of Coffee Bars
                      Praise him for the rattle of the pin table
                      Praise him for the chatter and the din
                      Praise him for the deep booming Juke Box
                      Praise him for the smoke and steam
                      Here the door is open
                      All may come in
                      And sit and talk, or smoke in silence
                      Watching, or being watched
                      Rub shoulders with the world
                      At peace with man
                      United in an enterprise
                      That makes an economic proposition
                      Out of generosity

There is no lock here
There is no garden gate
That makes of hospitality
A favoured gift
Bestowed upon the few
Here all are welcome
Provided that they pay
But since costs must be met
And nothing here is perfect
Let's thank God for Coffee Bars
Where we can meet
And be at home among our fellow men.
Teach us, Good Lord, to be more generous
Free us from the fear, the lack of trust
That alienates us from our fellow men
Teach us the meaning of forgiveness
To love our enemies
To welcome, as did Jesus
Those unlovely types
Whose pride, whose reputation, or whose smell
Makes them impossible
And since it is our sin to shut men out
By carelessness or wilful prejudice
Throw wide the door of our concern
To fight, to suffer and to care
With all who seek your Kingdom here on earth

A CONFESSION:

Reader: Lord we confess:
         That by silence and the ill-considered word
People: We have built up the walls of prejudice.

Reader: That by selfishness and lack of sympathy
People: We have stifled generosity.

Reader: That in thinking of our safety and reputation
People: We have passed by on the other side.

Reader: That by obsession with our own affairs
People: We have had no time for others.

Reader: For all our failures
People: Lord, forgive us.

Reader: And in thy mercy
People: Accept us, Good Lord, Amen.

Congregation: 'Blowin' in the Wind' (Bob Dylan)

FREEDOM AND FAITH

Reader:

God made man to be free
Free within the human family
The Commonwealth of man is still his dream

*Christ
shows the
way to
freedom
through
faith*

In Charter and in Constitution
In Petition and in Pact
He inscribes his faith
In Freedom and Equality
Yet still the barriers rise
And prejudice is strong
Fear and suspicion separate
And sever man from man

Why does the dream delay?
Why is hope unfulfilled?
Man lacks the faith
He lacks the faith of Christ
Who lived out his belief
Who in a hostile world
Revealed the potency of love
By this one act he realized the dream
And bridged the gap that separated man from man
The wall was down
And Jew and Gentile
Slave and free
Were one in Christ
So when men dare to love
They can release a power
That heals the sad divisions of mankind
Where men give up security and home
To help a backward people with their skills
There hope is born
Where statesmen patiently negotiate
And sacrifice advantage and prestige
There peace can grow
Where Negro kneels before the bullying guard
Immune to provocation and to hate
There love can heal
Where men will venture on a hope
Of truth and goodness yet untried
And take Christ at his word
There God can work.
Lord, give us faith.

    Luke 17: 5, 6
    James 1: 5-8
    Hebrews 11: 1, 8-10

Congregation: 'We shall Overcome'
(seated)

To COLONEL ALEXEI LEONOV:

Reader: So you stepped out of your space capsule
Into nothing
Where man had never been before
You hovered in a partial vacuum
Hazarding all upon a theory
No one had done before what you have done
No one could be quite sure what you would meet
Of course they made their calculations
Caution had carefully prepared for what might be
But no one could be sure
Until you clambered out
Man's dream remained
A wistful longing, unfulfilled
But you made out of it
Reality

And so you gave man freedom to explore
A medium beyond
The envelope of atmosphere, his home
New Worlds are his
Not only hemispheres
Infinities of space
With only time to check his wanderings
And all this came
From opening a door
And stepping into
The unknown

Lord make us men of faith
Faith to trust in what we hope for
Faith to live by what we cannot prove
until we risk ourselves upon it
With our lives

Teach us by man's conquest of the world
By those who ventured on a dream
And found new continents, new truth, new power
By faith
Teach us to trust the hopes we have been given
The hope of peace and welfare for mankind
The hope that love means more than hate
The hope that death is not the cynical denial
Of all that man has hoped for.

153

Teach us to take these and to live by them
And so to find that liberty from fear
And live as free men in a world
Where man is called to live by faith
Or to withdraw
A frightened beast, defeated by reality.

Teach us to live
As Jesus lives
Who took the hopes of men
And made them real
By stepping out of safe convention
Into love.

And so he gave us freedom
By his faith.

Congregation: Hymn No. 812
(Standing)

PRAYERS

Congregation: Hymn No. 249
(Standing)

BLESSING: The Lord bless you in the city and country
                        in home and street
                        in church and coffee bar
                        in suburb and down town
                        in school and leisure
                        in conversation and prayers.
             The grace of the Lord Jesus Christ
                        and the love of God
                        and the fellowship of the Holy Spirit
             be with us now and evermore.

People: AMEN.

Comments

1. The weakness of this service is obvious. It is conceived more as a performance than an act of worship. This may be explained by the fact that it was 'performed' in a Central Hall (Westminster, no less) to a congregation of a thousand or so senior pupils. It was prepared by various parties who did not meet until the day, so that the readings, the music and the preaching were never fully co-ordinated.

2. This does not excuse the fact that the readings, which are part discourse, part prayer, do not give room for much response. With

154

slight adaptations they could be divided up between the congregation and the readers. The clear lesson from all this is that adequate rehearsal and revision is essential.

3. The prayers obviously owe a great deal to Michel Quoist and show the possibilities of blank verse as a liturgical medium.

Further Comments
At times there is something artificial about this. Quoist was fresh and stimulating, but phrases like 'the dim and unreligious light of coffee bars' seem a mere striving after effect.

A FINAL COMMENT *Raymond George*

I am impressed by this wealth of experiment and encouraged to know that more is being done than I had realized. The deep concern at the state of the world is apparent: many of the services are a kind of propaganda, and this continues our emphasis in preaching and proclamation. The element of response is perhaps not so satisfactory. Though there is a good deal of spoken response, in addition to the traditional hymns, there is a certain tendency to write the responses in such a way as to 'get at' the congregation.

The common omission which I noted earlier, that of a great prayer of thanksgiving for creation and redemption at the climax of the service, is more than a matter of liturgical form. The theology of many of these services is more concerned with creation and (to some extent) incarnation than with cross and resurrection. There is some danger that the new secularization may be the old liberalism writ large: it would be a pity to lose sight of the emphasis of the intervening period of biblical theology on the mighty acts of God, in salvation-history.

But twenty years ago very few people thought of experiments of this kind, and my main feeling today is one of gratitude that we are living at the beginning of a creative period in the history of worship.

A Final Note
Recently an information service has been set up to provide a regular bulletin concerning experiments in worship, music, and liturgy, together with Visual Aid material. Because such information dates quickly we have not provided any here, but refer readers to this service which is supplied by Bernard Braley, 'Lornehurst', Belton, Great Yarmouth, Norfolk, at a cost of two shillings subscription per year.